CAMPING
LEADERSHIP
counseling
and programming

CAMPING LEADERSHIP

counseling and programming

MARIE D. HARTWIG
The University of Michigan
Ann Arbor, Michigan

BETTYE B. MYERS
Texas Woman's University
Denton, Texas

The C. V. Mosby Company
Saint Louis   1976

Library of Congress Cataloging in Publication Data

Hartwig, Marie.
    Camping leadership.

    Bibliography: p.
    Includes index.
    1. Camp counselors.   I. Myers, Bettye, joint
author.   II. Title.
GV198.C6H28   796.54′5   75-33168
ISBN 0-8016-2081-3

TS/S/B   9   8   7   6   5   4   3   2   1

preface

Camping Leadership: Counseling and Programming is designed to be used by young people interested in working with children in a resident camp setting. The format and content will be useful in the counselor-in-training programs that are conducted at actual campsites and that provide direct, daily contact with campers. The book will also be suitable for camping courses taught at the college or university level and for teachers and youth group leaders.

Our combined experience of over 60 years in leadership and administrative roles in resident camping have led us to the common philosophy that children are human—even at camp—and that a resident camp setting provides a marvelous, almost unparalleled, opportunity for the best and the worst in children and adults to rise to the surface. The child with a problem is indeed a problem child in a group setting and will continue to be so until the counselor can determine the cause of the problem and subsequently discover an appropriate means of diverting the camper's energies toward positive, acceptable patterns of behavior. It is our view that the majority of campers in our summer camps are *normal* children who demonstrate patterns of behavior that are normal but that nevertheless frequently puzzle the counselors who are trying to guide children in their maturational process.

The material selected for inclusion in the book represents two major categories: theoretical material regarding child development and program material for use with children in a resident camp setting. Selected and revised portions of the content from our out-of-print *Children Are Human—If the Counselor Really Knows Them* have been included where appropriate. The blank spaces throughout the book provide the reader with an opportunity to write in personal applications of the material covered.

We are indebted to many individuals with whom we have crossed paths throughout our many years of camping. It would not be possible to thank them all by name. We also extend our thanks to the hundreds of campers, counselors, and camp directors who have been patient with us while we learned. Specifically, we would like to express our indebtedness to two individuals who made so many learning opportunities possible: Dr. Joseph E. Maddy, the late founder and president of the National Music Camp, Interlochen, Michigan, and Miss Doris Johnson, owner and director of Camp Waldemar for Girls, Hunt, Texas. Our special thanks to Harlan Bloomer for his creative artwork used in the cover design and the opening figures for four parts of the book.

MARIE D. HARTWIG
BETTYE B. MYERS

contents

introduction

the challenge
of camping

In planning their sessions camp owners and directors have been aware of the educational aspects of camping. Many of them are teachers who hire senior staff with the "know how" to develop an enriching summer session.

Many of these key people work hard at keeping up with changing times and attitudes through reading, classes, travel, and by participating in the state, regional, and national meetings of the American Camping Association.

As specialized camps develop, which present further exposure in a particular field, the focus on "real camping" sometimes gets lost. The educational set of the city has too often just been moved into another environment—the woods. It was President Kennedy who managed to make the public aware of our disappearing natural resources—the shore lines, the forests, the breathing spaces. If we are fortunate enough to be in or near the woods, we should not ignore the opportunity to study and teach and learn in and about them. We venture to say that such education is a rare asset. Long-accepted theories of human nature have been shaken since the publication of books such as Robert Ardrey's *The Territorial Imperative*. We might even view our old haunts in the woods through different eyes than we have before. Or if we *have* used our eyes in the past, we will see what we saw in the past in greater depth, fortified by new understanding and new learning.

Our changing times have resulted in a "generation gap" that has caused concern to old and young alike. There has always been this gap, really, but modern innovations, affluence, and mobility will possibly lead to shifting values and attitudes.

In camping we need to provide leaders who are teachers in every sense of the word. To fill places for teachers, we have relied on willing young people a majority of whom have no intention of becoming teachers. As counselors, they are put in the position of helping

1

shape the camper's life, a task they perform with sincerity but often without the proper teaching tools. Bad experiences are bound to happen, and many of them can be written off by a trained counselor or teacher as the way "not to do it again." When these experiences are repeated through ignorance, there should be concern for the damage that might affect campers and staff alike.

Yes, we are leading up to the eternal question: Where and how does the camp director get trained personnel? Most must operate with a "do it yourself" kit. The director and top staff must develop an *ongoing, in-service* training program. This is not a preliminary that is completed three to five days before camp officially begins. It takes place in addition to *during* camp and is followed by bulletins during the year. This method of training puts a tremendous responsibility on the director and top staff. But, for the present and immediate future, in-service training is the only answer to the dilemma.

Adults in camping may feel that young people now interested in camping are not as dedicated as those who have been in it for many years. First of all, camping is not their main concern; second of all, the salaries have not kept up with the times, and the salary is rarely a drawing card. In spite of this, young people are willing to spend some time in the camping field, and it is our job to help them. These young people bridge the gap to the campers quickly, and they are capable of spotting needs and offering suggestions. And the adults in camping must keep up with the developments in group work, structuring, and planning. There *are* new methods, there *are* exciting developments, and there *are* new directions toward which we could look.

Directors are busy people. They are capable of responding to new and exciting ideas. They are human enough to admit to a love of the out-of-doors, to share their knowledge, and to be honest about their reactions. One such director anonymously turned in the following poem after a "working conference":

"The more we share, the greater we care."
This new perception is in the air.
It's been such fun to communicate
The interchange was really great.
We now are charged with motivation
To make camp more than a summer vacation.
We hope to hold this firm resolve
Our leadership to fully involve.
The more we share, the greater they care,
And if we don't, our leaders won't.
We now express appreciation
For what has been a "Revelation."

part I

the training ground
for counselors

Learn by doing

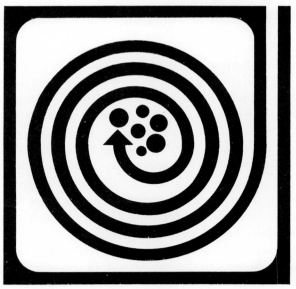

Counselor-in-training programs usually take place in either a university or camp setting. In a counselor training or counselor education program there are opportunities to study some of the problems in camping, to acquire skills essential in camp life, and to develop leadership in individual and group work. If the training cannot be conducted in a camp setting, a course on campus can be developed. The purpose of this program is (1) to help prepare future camp counselors; (2) to present a basic philosophy of camping and guidance; (3) to make participants aware of the aims and purposes of camping; (4) to equip participants with skills for group work; (5) to teach some of the essential skills associated with camping; (6) to provide teaching experience in many of these skills; and (7) to provide progressive experience in leadership work. Such a course should provide a plan of supervision and evaluation of internship for at least two different age groups. This workbook would be a useful part of the learning sessions.

The college- or university-based program can easily be developed jointly among several departments. The core of the program is found in the physical education department. Physical educators often state that their field does not cross over into camping and recreation. It is not that they are unwilling to incorporate these areas; it is simply that time does not permit. When it comes to hiring counselors to teach sport skills and dance, however, what age group responds to the call? College students! And which department is flooded with requests from camp directors? Physical education. The present great need for trained young people will get increasingly greater. The need could be at least partially met if the related areas of camping and recreation were combined in an orientation course. Young men in physical education have not been easily attracted to camping or recreation. And yet, for both the young men and women who are novice teachers, there is probably no better grounding in the profession than being a camp counselor who teaches young people through sports or dance. This experience, combined with cabin counseling, provides a living textbook. If there is a precamp session and continued in-service training, what better opportunity for prospective physical education teachers to practice what has been learned? A young person training to be a physical education teacher usually plans to work with children in a school system. The skills developed during such preparation include the skills used in camps, on the playground, and in situations generally termed recreation. Trained leadership in all of these ventures is hard to come by. Experts tell us that the demand for trained recreational leadership exceeds the supply. Recreation or physical education courses are the ones that more often than not provide prospective camp counselors in colleges and universities with leadership training. It would be most useful if college courses in camp counseling had an internship to accompany the theory portion of the camp counseling course. This internship must be with children. Depending upon the size of the city in which the college or university is located, college students could work with the city recreation program and conduct an activity or serve as assistants to a Brownie or Cub Scout troop. These college students should do volunteer work with children under the supervision of a wise and patient adult. In other words a camp counseling course must have a volunteer leadership outlet available during the academic year that is comparable to the student teaching experience. It is not adequate to teach the course in the spring semester, place students in counseling positions the following summer, and withhold credit for the course until the summer experience is completed. Teachers of camp counseling courses must be more ingenious than they have been in the past if they are going to do a good job in preparing physical education majors, sociology majors, elementary education majors, and others to be good camp counselors. Furthermore, college and university staffs should include individuals who have had recent camp experience. Unfortunately a person who has not set foot in a camp for years is sometimes assigned to teach the camp leadership course. Teachers must be abreast of current trends in camping. They should be required to be active members of their state and regional sections of the ACA.

A group of sophomore and junior men and women in a university class were asked to name the profession of the person who had influenced their life most in the last five years and to list the characteristics of this person. Out of twenty-seven possible choices, the teaching profession rated highest with eleven, coaching numbered four, the business profession rated three, another student was mentioned twice, a priest and a summer camp director were mentioned once, and fathers were mentioned three times. A glance at the descriptive words used by these young people reveals a great deal about their values. Of course, values vary according to individual experience, but the list nevertheless serves as a "sit up and take note" to all of us who work with young people. It shows the things that are important to them. The following qualities were mentioned first:

Understanding	Intelligence
Ability to teach	Kindness
Sensitivity to needs	Tolerance
Honesty	Confidence in me
Patience	Dynamic
Interest in each person	Concern for character
Strong character	Demanding of respect
Respect for others	Self-sufficiency
Sincerity	Ambition

These are key words for this age group, they are significant of the kind of attitudes these young people are forming, and we "old dogs" should take comfort in the fact that they are the kind of words they are. They represent the very qualities we are trying to pass on to campers. It is therefore not too demanding that the adult in camping is expected to be a paragon of virtue. And, strangely enough, when you know what is expected of you, it is easier to be that model. It is during precamp that first impressions are made by everyone about everyone. It should not be a hurried time fraught with pressures. Each one of the previously stated "quality words" needs *time* to develop, *time* to be observed, and *time* to be thought about.

Writing about a summer camp director, a young man listed the following qualities:
Patience
Understanding
Can make anyone feel at home right away
Always ready to help out
Organized
Able to control when control is called for
Sense of humor
A young woman described a staff person at camp with these phrases:
A sense of interest in each person she meets (I found out later she has a correspondence with over 100 people.)
A view of life with a Christian attitude
The ability to instill enthusiasm in others
The ability to share each emotion as another feels it
Those of us in camp leadership positions have a tremendous responsibility to live up to these observations.

The Counselor in Training (CIT) program in a camp setting is, of course, the preferred pattern. The proximity to all the components of camping—from observation and working with the campers to the acquisition of all the skills associated with camping—is ideal. Usually one member of staff is in charge of the CIT program. In some instances the CIT's are housed together; in others they work with a cabin counselor as an understudy. Activity heads assist in "building" these trainees. This shared plan of training calls for a cooperation among all staff members, which can result in a cohesiveness most beneficial to the total camp.

Supervision and evaluation of CIT's

The setup in which class work is combined with the immediate opportunity to use and to observe the use of newly acquired knowledges and skills is the core of the entire training program. Living in a cabin, eating with the campers, being a part of the formal and informal recreational program, and being included in staff meetings gives the CIT a total picture of the counselor's job. The isolated knowledges and skills learned in class fall into a meaningful pattern when direct application is observed. The eight-week camp period calls for continued and steady awareness of the CIT's growth and for a plan of evaluation.

The total staff must, of course, be aware of the counselor-in-training program and sympathetic to it. Persons assisting in the evaluation of another individual cannot help but take stock of themselves. The process can be a force of upgrading for the entire staff. The form for evaluating should be designed carefully. Using checklists and numerical or letter grades without providing an opportunity to amplify the point of view results in spur-of-the-moment decisions that lack careful analysis. A suggested form is on p. 7. The following is a suggested plan for its use in an eight-week program:

1. Discuss the purpose of evaluation with CIT's, as well as with camp personnel.
2. Ten days into the camp season, have the CIT take the form to the counselor, who should fill it out in pencil and discuss it with the CIT.
3. The fourth week of the camp season the counselor completes the final report. Administrative personnel concerned fill out a similar form, as does the supervisor.
4. At the end of the fourth week, the counselor, the director, and the supervisor of the CIT's conduct a personal interview with the CIT. All report forms should be available. The three people who are in the best position to assist a CIT are present to encourage the trainee and to make suggestions for improvement. The camp setting itself should promote a friendly and informal tone for the interview. For many CIT's this experience is the first face-to-face discussion of themselves and their progress with sympathetic, understanding adults.
5. Repeat this procedure for the last four weeks of internship experience even if the CIT group is not new.
6. An accumulative record sheet can show the total ratings at a glance.

COUNSELOR EDUCATION PROGRAM
Evaluation of the CIT

NAME OF CIT_____ Date_____

This sheet will become a part of the CIT's permanent record. As a technique of guidance, your rating will be shared with the CIT during a private interview with his or her faculty advisor. Please be frank and honest in your appraisal. Remember—a rating based on bias of any kind is of NO value to the CIT or to your division.

DIRECTIONS: Please assign the numerical symbol that best describes the individual's rating in each category. You *Expand on each rating* in the space provided by giving examples of observed behavior that will support your rating and help to convey your impressions. If you are unable to make a judgment on a specific statement, please place a check in the "Don't know" column.

Ratings: 1—Outstanding   2—Creditable   3—Acceptable   4—Poor   5—Detrimental

	Rating	"Don't know"
1. Understands basic motives, needs, and problems of campers.		
2. Is sympathetic and helpful to "difficult" campers as well as "good" campers.		
3. Maintains unemotional and objective attitudes toward undesirable conduct of campers.		
4. Has the confidence and respect of the campers.		
5. Helps to foster a good group relationship with the children.		
6. Treats all campers with equal courtesy and respect and shows no favorites.		
7. Works well with divisional counselor staff.		
8. Demonstrates qualities of dependability.		
9. Has the personality for group work with children.		
10. Has shown evidence of personal maturation during past four weeks.		

Would you recommend that this CIT be rehired next year as a counselor? __Yes, without reservation; __Yes, with reservation; __ No. (Use back of page to give reasons for your decision.)

Signed _____

Position _____

CIT EVALUATION SUMMARY SHEET

Name_____ Date_____

Key: 1—Outstanding   2—Creditable   3—Acceptable   4—Poor   5—Detrimental

Trait	1st four weeks_____ Age group_____			2nd four weeks_____ Age group_____		
	Counselor	Director	Supervisor	Counselor	Director	Supervisor
1. Motives, needs						
2. Sympathetic						
3. Unemotional						
4. Confidence						
5. Group relations						
6. No favorites						
7. Divisional staff						
8. Dependability						
9. Personality						
10. Maturation						
Rehire? Yes, without reserva- tion						
Yes, with reservation						
No						

Comments

Final recommendation for hiring:
    Yes
    No

_____
Head of Department

part II

camp management

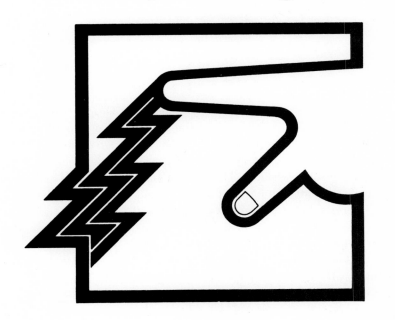

Organization and administration

There are as many camp designs as there are directors or owners. Over the years the placement of living units, whether tents or cabins, has been less formal and militaristic. Thus, informal units or groupings are easily formed into small communities. These units can be self-contained, to the point of including programming.

Charts depicting "chain-of-command" design should be so simple that a hierarchy is not established. All jobs should take into consideration the good of the camper. Camp cannot escape being an educational agency. Learning opportunities abound in all sorts of areas. All "departments" exist to maintain and create new opportunities. One mental image could be that of a wheel with the camper as the hub from which the spokes emanate. Another image could be that the pie-shaped pieces formed by the spokes are areas that point to the camper. One student described the camp as a cell with the camper as the core.

Whatever the administrative design, it is important for it to show functions rather than titles and peoples' names. Too much hierarchy increases the time necessary for decision making. Draw a chart depicting the organizational structure of your camp. Try to be "original."

Every camp should have a list of objectives. Despite the seeming informality of most camp situations, objectives can only be accomplished through an educational approach. In camp there are many opportunities to learn through doing. The objectives (whether they are in print or not) can be sorted into two groups. One group will be *specific* to the particular camp; the other group will be *basic* to most camps. If the objectives within each area are attained, the outcome for each camper should be an enjoyable experience, good health, new interests, more and improved skills, a satisfying experience in group living, an appreciation for nature, and a spiritual enrichment from all associations.

In recent years some of the following trends have become evident in camping. Many have had marked effect on camp organization. (1) It has become educational; (2) leadership training is recognized as important; (3) it has become decentralized; (4) year-round school camps are developing; (5) camping is being used for specific purposes; (6) there is flexibility in programs; (7) environment studies have been introduced; (8) campcraft and woodcraft are emphasized; (9) more time is spent in training counselors; (10) it has developed CIT programs with or without college credit; (11) more young people are seeking employment since the age of majority was reduced to eighteen; (12) camp organization is more democratic; (13) family camping has become organized; and (14) more middle aged and older people are interested in camping.

The basic structure of a camp can be decentralized or highly organized, but there are a few areas that remain constant no matter what the organization. These are the program, food, health, business, and maintenance. These areas are held together by the director. The area heads are the program director, dietician, physician or nurses, business manager, and caretaker. If the camp is broken into smaller living communities, these units are generally known to the camper by a name (person, tribe, animal, bird, and so on), a number, or age grouping, such as junior or intermediate.

The assistant director usually heads the program area, and is assisted by activity heads or activity specialists who may or may not have cabin duties. A good training plan is to have understudies or assistants to the activity heads or specialists.

The counselor is in more direct contact with the camper. Part III is devoted to the counselor's role. The CIT is an understudy for the position of counselor and perhaps for another position of responsibility in the camp organization.

There are also many young people who are not quite old enough to be hired as counselors, but who assume such jobs as dish washer, kitchen help, and so on in order to be part of a camp organization.

All camps in this country have ties to sponsoring agencies or to other directors, such as those in private organizations. The ACA has provided direction toward the best there can be in camping for all types of camps and has adopted a symbol, the acorn, to be used by member camps in good standing. Camps accredited through inspection by the ACA are permitted to use an especially designed acorn seal in their promotional work. The ACA will be discussed later in the text.

The ACA also makes allowance for grass roots contributions and local committee work. Conferences held at state, regional, and national levels provide the basic structure for exchange. Special services are offered to members, and, as expansion takes place, additional services will be available to the membership. Directors and counselors could and should hold memberships and take active part in the year-round activities of the Association. Membership in ACA means affiliation with a mutual and "going" concern.

Staff

Necessary preparations for the "summer menu" are planned with the needs and interests of the campers in mind. Records from the previous summer give the director ideas as to which "dishes" were the most popular and which ones need a change of ingredients. The ingredients that must go into the creation of a successful camp season are many and varied. They include the entire camp staff, the campers, the facilities, and the weather, to name but a few.

Since the success of the "meal" depends to a large extent upon the quality of the individuals comprising the counseling staff, it is well to consider the thoughts that might run through the director's mind when the counselors are first assembled during precamp. In cookbook terminology the director would first of all look the ingredients over to discover any bad spots such as spoilage or mold. Are they in the amounts contracted for? Are the skins too thick? Are any of the ingredients usable just as they are or must some of them be cooked (if so, for how long?). Should they be simmered, brought to a boil, or are they just as well off half-baked? Are the ingredients fresh, or are some left over from last year? How were the particular brands selected? Were they easily available this year? Through scarcity of the item, was it necessary to accept some off-brands? How many years has each brand been on the market? Just how will each ingredient affect the planned menu?

Substituting the word counselor for the word ingredient gives an indication of the problem that may confront the director when planning precamp and in-service training sessions. How much help each counselor will need depends to a large extent upon the selection process the director has followed in hiring counselors. The more nearly the director has been able to hire counselors who share and believe in ACA objectives, the easier the job will be to train individuals to be useful members of the counseling team.

The camp director

Who is a camp director? A member of the human species or a relative of the octopus family? Sometimes members of the camp staff have difficulty determining the appropriate category. Directors demonstrate many qualities of each species. They are friendly, concerned with the welfare of each member of the camp family, sensitive to the praise and criticism heaped upon the camp, get tired and occasionally irritable, and once in a while even succumb to a short-tempered remark. In other words they seem almost human. On the other side of the ledger they get involved in so many little "this-and-thats" that they appear to have their hands in at least eight different things all at the same time. In this they more closely resemble the octopus.

Directors must be all things to all people, or so it seems. They must entice campers to enroll, convince parents that they will get their money's worth because Johnny or Susy will return home with good character traits and good social habits such as table manners and tidiness. The next step is to search through the labor pool and hire counselors who can make this promise to the parents become a reality. This is just the beginning.

Whether directors actually do the work themselves or hire someone else to do some of the tasks, they are responsible for making sure that the camp facilities are as safe and free from hazards as possible, the equipment is available and in good repair for use at the opening of the camp, the maintenance men follow the correct specifications in laying out the tennis courts, the roofs of the cabins or tents do not leak, and each dwelling has its own wastebasket, mop, and broom. If it is a girls' camp, the director must worry about laundry facilities and attempt to persuade a local laundry that the girls will not complain too much if their blouses and shorts shrink. If it is a boy's camp, arrangements have to be made for regular haircut time and for those who use electric razors to scrape off the "peach fuzz." Proper insurance coverage, adequate medical facilities, a sanitary kitchen, and the operational budget are all worries that directors must struggle with before, during, and after camp closes. To return to the original question, "Who is a camp director?" The answer is simple: a human being who is sometimes willing to behave as an octopus because of strong beliefs in the values of camping for children. This is a person who is willing and able to tackle all of the previously mentioned tasks and hundreds of others to develop an organization capable of providing countless opportunities for children, counselors, and himself to become better human beings.

In spite of the many "octopus duties," camp directors are also responsible primarily for the human quality of counseling that is done by the members of staff. It is physically impossible to meet personally the physical, psychological, and social needs of each camper. Directors must be able to rely on counselors to meet these immediate needs and must use every means available to insure that counselors are adequately prepared to respond to parents' rightful demand for counselors who are fully informed of the characteristics of the age group with whom they are working and who are sensitive to the children's problems.

Finding such individuals is difficult, and if a large staff is needed, the problem is compounded. The success of the camp season for the campers will depend upon the quality of the staff chosen. Young men and women who are *child-centered* rather than self-centered or activity-centered individuals will contribute much more to the camping experience. The extra dollars it may cost to secure such counselors is the best investment that can be made. The finest tennis courts, horses, diving boards, or sailboats are of little value if the counselors are unable to help a child who is homesick, has bad table manners, is offensive with personal habits, cries during sleep, or knows only aggressive behavior as a technique for securing attention and affection. Ideally, the director should be the one best qualified to assist counselors to understand and successfully work with the campers. The director should be as free as possible from "octopus duties" in order to be readily available to counselors for guidance. If the director cannot take this responsibility, there *must* be someone on the administrative staff who is qualified to do so.

It is the director's responsibility to provide a precamp training program that is meaningful and beneficial to "oldtimers" as well as to newcomers on the counseling staff. Likewise, it is an urgent responsibility to maintain a worthwhile in-service training program throughout the camp session, devoted primarily to understanding the needs and problems of children. When one considers the duties and responsibilities of a camp director, one cannot help but be amazed that a human being in his "right mind" would eagerly seek such a role. Fortunately, hundreds of men and women do assume such roles.

The counselor

Who or what is a camp counselor? Some of his noncamping friends might say, "He is a fool." Perhaps they are correct. Many campers say, "He's the swellest person in the world"; and others will say the opposite—"He's the lousiest." The camp director may describe the counselor as a "gem" or as a "mistake."

Which label fits the best? The answer lies in the counselor's reasons for accepting a camp job, his general attitude about children and adults, and his behavior while at camp. It is foolish to assume the job will be a vacation or a means of getting rich. Friends at home will probably make far more money at the factory, store, as a secretary or doing road work and will not have the responsibilities and worries that come with a camp job. It is unfortunately true that good camp counselors are generally shamefully underpaid. Taking all these disadvantages into consideration, perhaps the counselor *is* a complete fool to accept a job in a summer camp, particularly if he does not love children.

If the counselor is to be accorded the "the swellest person" label by campers, however, he must have more than a love for children. The counselor must also understand the age characteristics of the campers. Such an understanding involves more than a textbook knowledge of children. The counselor must be able to apply "theory" material to the flesh and blood complexities of each individual child. How often have camp directors heard inexperienced counselors comment that children don't respond or behave as the "book" said they would? Perhaps these counselors neglected to read the fine print, which indicated that in general certain physical, psychological, or social characteristics appear in an orderly fashion and at predetermined periods during the maturation process, but that individuals *vary* in this maturation rate. To repeat, camp counselors must understand and be sensitive to the age characteristics and needs that result from accelerated, normal, or retarded developmental stages of a child's maturation. The counselor has the right to expect the camp director to assist him in this endeavor.

The counselor will likely be called upon to substitute for the camper's parents, dog, cat, bird, grandmother or grandfather, uncle, aunt, brother or sister, or even pet hamster. Certainly the counselor will represent security for each child. Furthermore, he must be willing to accord each camper as much or more understanding, patience, kindness, forgiveness, and opportunity for second chances that he desires for himself.

The counselor's relationship with other adults at camp is an important factor in determining the director's evaluation of him. In relationships with parents counselors must keep

13

in mind the stark truth that parents have certain rights and privileges in regard to their children, whether the counselor approves or not. For example, parents may ship their unwilling child off to camp so that they may have a vacation. At home the parents may choose to have the child eat in the kitchen with the hired help more often than in the dining room with them. They may in many ways be depriving the child of warm affection even though they are showering him with expensive, impractical gifts. It could very well be that such parental behavior may be contributing to the child's problem of adjustment at camp, but it is not the responsibility of the counselor to "straighten out" the parents by letter or through face-to-face conversation when the parents come to visit at camp. Opportunities may arise that will provide the counselor with a chance to offer suggestions to the parents. Before making recommendations of a personal nature, the counselor should discuss them at length with the camp director since in general the counselor's job is to work with children, not reform parents.

Staff morale is another important determinant of the success of a camp season. It is not necessary for staff members to be extremely close to one another, but it is essential that each person be able to work well with each member of the camp staff. A good working atmosphere is the responsibility of each counselor and of the entire administrative staff. It may mean that the counselor will need to put his own wants and wishes aside momentarily if they are not compatible with the philosophy or policies of the camp. The counselor's attitude toward other adults in the camp and his relationships with them will be important factors in the director's evaluation of him.

Is the camp counselor a fool? If it is foolish to love children, to want to work with them on a twenty-four hour day basis in spite of low pay, to enjoy the companionship of other adults who share a dedication to the values of camping, to cherish such titles as "the swellest person in the world," then we must conclude that a camp counselor is a fool. But, we may be sure that this "fool" is happy in the knowledge that as a camp counselor he has shared the responsibility for helping shape the life of a human being.

The camper

Who and what is a camper? Who knows? It depends upon which child we are discussing. The camper may be a dirty-fingernailed girl who spends all of her free time trying to catch snakes. Or it may be an eight-year-old fellow who is very much afraid of insects. We might mean the teenage boy or girl who is searching for the answer to, "Who am I?" We could talk about the youngster who was sent to a special camp at the request of his psychiatrist because he knew that the camp staff was adequately prepared to follow through the treatment program necessary. Or, the camper could be the handicapped youngster with cerebral palsy. It is almost impossible to select a single set of characteristics that adequately describe all the campers who attend summer camp. To be entirely accurate, our description of a camper is limited to the following statement: A camper is a human being who possesses physical, psychological, and social characteristics that determine his attitude and behavior in a myriad of circumstances. To understand and work with the camper, the counselor must know the camper well enough to determine what makes him or her uniquely different from all the other campers. In the chapters that follow, the counselor will be exposed to a variety of techniques that can be used to achieve this goal.

Children *are* human, if the counselors really know them. Knowing them is more than knowing a name or nickname, sound of voice, color of hair, and whether they have a buddy. Knowing them implies a knowledge of the characteristics of the particular age group. Knowing them is a continuous process. Each day is full of opportunities for developing understanding between camper and counselor. Each day provides examples of maturation, maintenance of the status quo, or regression in the camper. The wide awake counselor will observe these opportunities and will get to know the camper.

With full knowledge of the unique characteristics of each camper, the counselor will find planning cabin events a real pleasure and will no longer dread a class that includes a camper with a problem. Knowing the campers means being prepared and not being thrown by certain camper reactions. It means expecting these reactions, being ready for them, and having them occur (if they cannot be forestalled) with the least amount of damage to the group or the camper. Knowing children sometimes means letting certain things happen as a matter of learning and maturation. Knowing them means appreciating all the goodness in each camper and seeking opportunities for it to be expressed. Knowing them implies that the counselor who is not in a position to handle a situation will seek advice or turn the matter over to a better-qualified person. Knowing them involves loving, respecting, and supporting them in their endeavors. It also requires an adult capacity to pull something out of memory to explain a child's reaction. One such personal experience is that of the first airplane ride taken by two boys with their parents in a friend's plane. The day was bright, and the blue sky was filled with big white popcorn clouds. While passing through one of these clouds, the five-year-old peered out and asked, "Where's God?" His mother, feeling a bit squeamish from the ride, said, "Did you expect to see Him up here?" The boy replied, "Yeah, I thought He was up here making people." The baffled silence was broken by the boy's next question, "Well, if He's not here, where is Jack in the Beanstalk?" To most people this would be just another child's story. But an understanding in the mother and the aunt led to a search through one of the child's books, which revealed a full, borderless page of blue sky with Jack climbing up his beanstalk straight toward the top of the page—right through a white popcorn cloud!

Knowing children means all this and much more. As the counselor lives and works with the campers, he is in a sense working with clay, in that he has an opportunity to mold a child in many ways. He can bring out a sense of humor, instill a love for nature, create a pattern for goodness, and impart the desire for good sportsmanship. The counselor can recognize the struggle within a camper who is trying to do the "right thing." As he catches the camper's eye, no word need be spoken to communicate the understanding of a brief moment.

Gwen Frostic, the noted northern Michigan artist and writer, has thrilled many readers with her striking sketches of nature, which reveal her feeling for texture and color. From the winking toad to the feather drifting in the wind, *A Walk With Me* stirs the heart of the lover of nature. In her book, *These Things Are Ours*, she takes the reader one step further and places the responsibility to see beauty squarely upon each of us. A picture of beauty draws immediate response; seeing the real thing often leaves us without words equal to expressing how we feel. So it is with feelings between counselor and camper. When a moment of understanding occurs, there is no need for words.

In *Man and Leisure* Charles K. Brightbill discusses the needs that must be met to produce happiness. Not a narrow or limited happiness, but the happiness of a rewarding, enriched, and expressive existence. He tells us if we are not happy, it is because we do not know where to look for it or because we do not love life enough!"

Does the camp counselor know himself well enough and love life enough to be of help to others? The enthusiasm to find new patterns for living has to come from within a person. Although he can learn from others, the counselor must take responsibility for his own attitudes. He in turn must present desirable patterns for young people, the campers. They will see these patterns and select for themselves. This is why adults working with children must love life. The counselor can only show the camper by example; the doing must come from within the camper.

Hero worship is more conspicuous during childhood and early adolescence. Perhaps this is due to the fact that at this age young people have a great zest for life and living. In selecting their patterns they are openly worshipful of the person whose image reflects a way of life attractive to them. What happens to this love of life in the rest of us? Does age mean giving up striving for higher goals or for enjoying beauty? After a person reaches maturity, it is important to retain a young-in-heart quality.

One of the most giving persons known to us was a woman in her seventies, a teacher by trade, who dropped anything she was doing to give time to any child or adult, no matter what it was they asked. In a few short weeks at camp she was able to transmit a love for life in one small boy. His mother wrote that the boy had gone off to school in the fall with a light in his eye and a spring in his step. This sensitive teacher secretly hoped that the teacher taking over would keep this "light" and "spring" going.

At the other end of the age scale, a nineteen-year-old who was helping an underprivileged group of young children was so excited she pleaded with her classmates to come do the same—it was the most worthwhile thing she had ever done! This young woman had just discovered she could give to others and, furthermore, that they wanted and needed what she could give. Her love for life has increased measurably. The children who rubbed shoulders with these two adults have had their lives enriched beyond measure. What great need there is in camping for more adults of this kind.

Staff training
Precamp training

Counselor preparation takes place in many ways. Many people think of precamp work as taking place just prior to the opening of camp and, more often than not, at the camp site. Any communication, whether written or verbal, which takes place prior to the opening day of camp should be considered as precamp orientation or training. The following are examples of such training:

Correspondence with director
Correspondence with director and referral to the staff member heading the area in which the counselor will be working
Meetings during year with director
Meetings during year with person heading an area
Brochures
Manuals
Guide sheets
Previous reports
Sessions in camp before arrival of campers (usually referred to as precamp)

Preparation should be constant and should start before the counselors arrive at camp. If the counseling staff is drawn from a centralized geographical area, it is often possible for the entire group to get together during the winter or spring for planning and training sessions. Well spaced and planned meetings can whet the appetites of new counselors and arouse nostalgia for the camp opening before the snow has left the ground or the blue-bonnets and Indian paintbrush start to bloom. Returning counselors relish the opportunity to help in the training of new personnel. Such get-togethers help to solidify their own thinking as they help pass on important tips to the newcomers.

If the camp draws its personnel from a wide geographic area, getting together during the spring becomes impossible because of time and expense. The brochure advertising the camp does not always give all of the information the counselor wants or should have. Under such circumstances the use of some kind of manual is imperative. Many camp directors who go to the bother and expense of printing a camp manual and sending it to counselors after they sign their contract, fail to utilize the manual during precamp and throughout the course of the camp session. If the manual is worth the time and expense necessary for its publication and distribution, then it should be used to chart the course throughout the entire summer's journey. Failure to use the manual in this fashion makes it difficult to justify having one.

Many counselors focus on salary and time off prior to the actual signing of their contracts. *Before that signing* they should also know the objectives of the camp, its location, its typical terrain and weather, places available during time off periods, and the opportunities for training before or during the summer. Written reports or outlines that were developed by the person filling the position the previous year may constitute the training program. The counselor should know if there are traditions to surmount or adhere to. How much camper planning and suggestion is possible? How much is encouraged? Many of these issues deserve time to be mulled over—more time than is possible in a few days training at most precamp sessions.

There are many "thinking times" in the life of persons going to camp. During the day when one is alone, thoughts do come to mind—possibly stimulated by the title of a book at hand or seen in the bookstore window. If the counselor is a college student in education and is practice teaching, a new game, a different method of presentation, a clever bulletin board, or an expression from some child could be the seed of something different for camp. Discussing camp with fellow students and the resultant exchange of ideas is another kind of "learning times."

Directors would do well to recommend one or two favorite books on child development, articles published in the ACA monographs, current literature designed especially for women or men, sports publications, and home improvement magazines. The last three types of magazines have long recognized the need to constructively fill leisure hours and suggest all sorts of ways to do so—some of which can be applied to a camping situation. Which games can be done in a small space? Is there a multiple "space use" plan? What are some of the simple crafts? Are expensive craft materials necessary? What are the newest books on children's reading lists? Which books received awards? What are the old favorites? Do you know Mr. Toad? Charlotte? Eeyore? What is the name of the latest astronaut? What did he do?

An organized method of study and training should be used as a workbook. A look ahead to the camp period is important.

Precamp sessions *conducted on the camp site* vary in length, depending upon the size of the group, the training that has taken place before arrival, and the amount of time and money the director can afford to put into the meetings. Time lengths vary from one day to a full week for the precamp session. The longer the session, the greater the outcomes that may occur if the days are well planned and utilized.

In the past precamp sessions have been used to put the camp in physical readiness. Questions always arise as to how much labor counselors should be expected to expend in maintenance chores in getting the camp ready for opening day, particularly since wages for manual labor are generally much higher than counselors' salaries. The major allotment of the counselor's time during precamp should be used for discussion and study in preparation for working with the campers and conducting the program for the summer. In recent years directors have also utilized the precamp period for the development of cohesiveness among the staff. At camp an *esprit de corps* can be developed, the likes of which is hard to find in other settings.

In most camps the pressure and hurry of urban living is removed. People take one another at face value. They love the out-of-doors, there is time to stop and look, to take an extra deep breath for the fun of it, to look back to see where one has been and if one has really enjoyed it. And there is time to do it again! Precamp also gives the director an opportunity to observe a counselor's skills and vice versa.

To determine the length of the session, directors should plan an outline of steady work with enough time out for a recreational period each day. An orderly approach to the dissemination of ideas and materials can be more meaningful if different methods are used each day. The exciting approaches resulting from recent research in group dynamics give a new shine to the old shoe. Everyone has a share in the doing and it is stimulating to be a part of a living philosophy. For fun's sake, the counselors might stay in one or two cabins during precamp to get to know one another better. If time allows, an overnight, including a cookout, could be a high spot. It is times like these, singing around glowing campfire coals, that group morale grows, and the line that separated the new counselors from the old disappears. A sense of belonging often results from these fun times. There is no doubt that a good precamp session can make the individual evaluate himself and want to reach a little higher, to set a better example, and to help lead the way.

The appetizer—getting acquainted

During precamp, the old and new counseling staff have ample opportunity to become more at ease with one another, to be able to call one another by name, and to have a fairly good idea of the responsibilities of each. Many devices may be employed to facilitate this "getting to know you" process. Name tags during precamp are a real asset, and they save embarrassment for old and new staff members. Small group projects and prearranged meal partners go a long way to make a new counselor feel part of the group. If the truth be known, there are many homesick counselors among new staff members the first few days at camp. Such a situation is more likely to exist if there is a large number of returning staff members. It is extremely difficult for a new counselor to find his niche and to feel comfortable, wanted, and needed unless extra effort is expended during those first hours and days to dispel fears and feelings of insecurity. If the director does not have the time for this necessary task, he should delegate the responsibility to seasoned staff members. It must be done by someone—it will not just come about.

Getting acquainted includes getting to know the campers before they arrive at camp. During precamp counselors must have time to digest reports from the previous summer on returning campers and to familiarize themselves with the application blanks and records available on new campers. This can be an exciting time for counselors, and they should have an adequate amount of uninterrupted time to devote to it.

The main course—counseling techniques

The success of the entire menu is dependent upon the main course—counseling techniques. Because of its importance, another section, which could be studied during precamp and throughout the entire summer in-service training sessions, is devoted to a discussion of counseling techniques.

The salad—activities on land

Counselors who will be involved with land sports and crafts have areas and projects of their own that need to be studied. Counselors need to explore the woods ahead of time. Favorite campsites must be shared. The staff should examine the equipment to be used, put it into working order, and store it for easy summer use. Heads of sports activities need to meet with their helpers to go over safety factors and rules to be followed. Procedures in case of accident need to be learned ahead of time, even though *prevention* is automatically built into the planning. Simple procedures can be printed and distributed. A discussion of the reasons for any procedure is warranted if a question arises. Each of us in camping has had to come up the ladder rung by rung. If we think back, there were many times when we wondered and were afraid to ask for fear of showing ignorance about something we guessed we were supposed to know. Consequently, we took on the role of "pretenders." Luckily, in most cases, we were the only ones who were hurt by it, but it is possible that someone else might have been hurt through our ignorance. Hurt by those who are supposed to know! Counselors should be encouraged to question why if they do not understand. They must know if they are to be able to interpret and relate to campers.

Land sports and crafts will be discussed in more detail in a later section entitled Method of Serving.

The dessert—special events

There is a whole area of special events. Some of these are the traditions of the camp—special campfire ceremonies, show-off days for parents, water shows, carnivals, dramatic productions, special trips—those special occasions that perhaps happen only once during the camp season. Such occasions require discussion, preparation, and the eager help of new staff. These events are superimposed upon the regular camp programs and help to make each camp different from all others.

The new staff should learn the camp songs that are traditional to the camp. The new camper should never suspect the counselor is new, too.

Rainy days create a need for substitute activities. By the same token, a complete day of rest or quiet activities should be considered when excessive heat or fatigue has set in. A late reveille and breakfast never ruined a camp program, but its effect on the program needs to be anticipated during precamp planning.

These discussions sharpen counselor awareness and increase the counselors' respect for each other's skills. Each counselor will want to pull his own weight—and be a constructive member of the staff. It is only when inadequacies are allowed to fester that we find a breakaway individual or clique.

The beverage—waterfront activities

Success in this area lies in complete respect for waterfront rules and regulations and for the counselor in charge. Young counselors are not always aware of the responsibility that belongs to the person on duty at the waterfront. That person should be highly qualified and may have to risk his own life to save that of another. Time for serious discussion and questions and answers regarding waterfront procedures should be included in precamp. Part of the discussion should involve the entire camp staff, whether they are serving on the waterfront or not. All camp personnel must know the regulations and adhere to them. On days off the same rules should apply, and counselors should practice safety rules while recreating and swimming in nearby waters. *"That They May Live,"* a Red Cross film on mouth-to-mouth resuscitation, is an excellent color film demonstrating the use of mouth-to-mouth resuscitation in emergencies other than waterfront emergencies. Waterfront counselors and "landlubbers" who have seen this film recommend it highly as a *must* for everyone to see during precamp. A rerun for the campers should also be considered.

This wonderful area, the waterfront, deserves precamp time since it is one of the campers' favorites. Time spent planning for accident prevention and in establishing model behavior in the use of the waterfront will help set up a safe pattern for others to follow. Additional waterfront information is included in a later section.

In the growth and development of the ACA the basic objectives have increased in number; others have been refined or redefined. They represent the work of many people who are truly dedicated to camping. Counselors are not always aware of the camp's underlying roots. Nor are they always aware of the great responsibility reflected in final decisions the director makes.

There is no better way to *ruin* the precamp session than to devote the major portion of the time to the housekeeping chores of daily living—how to handle the laundry, writing letters to parents, and how to get necessary supplies are items of information that can be obtained from printed sheets or as the need arises. Sometimes new counselors are so saturated with this kind of information they completely forget that the camp is run for campers. A good camp manual can dispense with the need to discuss this kind of information.

The last night of precamp should provide everyone with a good night's sleep before the arrival of the campers. It is a director's dream to have each member of the staff eager to have the campers arrive because they are prepared, rested, and at ease.

One final issue deserves consideration by the director if counselors and campers are to receive maximum benefit from a summer camp program. How can camp directors answer the charges that are too often leveled at organized camping by people who look down their noses at camping and its programs? Such people claim the intellectual level of the programs is low. Those of us who know and love camping rise immediately in defense because the charge does not fit the camping we know. What we must face squarely, however, is the fact that the people who want to help us in camping are young, comparatively inexperienced, and in need of guidance. The young ones are not versed in the art of adult giving nor can they always be adult in receiving. But what they do give should be the best that is within their power to give. Adults should expect the best from them and help them to give it. Experienced staff and directors should ask themselves if they encourage counselors and campers to realize their full potential. In camping there are so many opportunities that never present themselves in the classrooms of grade schools, high schools, or colleges. Living twenty-four hours a day with one another in kindness and understanding, sharing the wonders of nature, and acquiring skills is not an experience that can be achieved through formal education.

Directors would also do well to read John Gardner's *Excellence*. After reading it, they would tackle the precamp program stimulated by the desire to prove that all education is not formal and that camping can provide a place of continuous learning throughout the life of an individual.

Camp directors are affectionately described as members of the octopus family in *Children ARE Human: If the counselors Really Know Them*, Volume 3. Their many duties make them "appear to have their hands in eight different things at the same time."

Methods of handling these "different things" do not arise from a moment's whim but are based on firm foundations strengthened by each year of experience.

In-service training

Training that takes place during the camp season is called in-service training. It may take the form of staff meetings, individual or small group conferences, after-taps discussions, available library and resource materials, visiting specialists, study groups, or parent seminars.

The sharing that can take place among staff *during* the season is often lost in the pressure of carrying out the camp season. Times are rare or nonexistent during a season when the camp personnel can meet *in one group* for this sharing. Heads of sport activities can share with their "teachers," unit heads with their counselors, the dietician with the food staff, and so on, but there is little opportunity for exchanges between areas. There is a common denominator to each area. Understanding the whys and wherefores of another area makes a person a more effective group member. Knowledge of another area need not be in great depth, but techniques used in one area can apply to another. Ongoing communication can result in a cohesiveness that cannot be accomplished in precamp.

Most camps provide an opportunity for parents to visit. Meeting with them to share ideas, suggestions, or to further inform is an advantage to all concerned. The written word is often misunderstood or needs amplification.

At the end of camp, reports on each area will assist the director in preparing for the following summer. There will undoubtedly be many suggestions from staff as the result of the opportunity to share in in-service training. The training program also needs planning—it does not just happen. If one person cannot direct it, a committee might. A design of some kind should be set, but requests from staff members should be incorporated. A time schedule will have to be flexible. Some groups will want to get together regularly and often. Others may want to get together weekly or every other week. The plan should meet the staff's needs.

A good in-service training program could result in better counselor return and lessen the pressure of the precamp session. Counselor turnover will determine the length and importance of precamp and will also affect the amount of stress in in-service training. Every director hopes to accomplish a little more each year. A plateau could last for several years if the staff has to be *trained* before and during camp.

In developing leaders it is important to keep in mind the process involved. "The responsibilities of a leader are to affect the course of events and to help each group member reach his maximum potential. A leader is not a teacher. A teacher imparts skills, while a leader imparts values. A counselor must be both teacher and leader. Leadership may not always be directed toward positive goals; the influence exerted on the group member may be in the direction of negative goals. Nevertheless, it is still leadership.

Current research in camping has shown that no single characteristic determines success as a counselor, except that the ability to work with others seems to be a fairly common trait among successful counselors.

Camping is in the business of character building and transmitting values. College courses cannot adequately prepare counselors to meet the needs of camps. The camp director should view leadership training as an ongoing process in his camp in order to prepare counselors to meet the specific demands of the camp setting in which they will be working."*

---

*Dr. Bettye Myers at the opening session of the Camp Directors' Institute, 1966.

Supervision and evaluation

In educational jargon the word supervision generally is associated with student teaching. The supervisor is the college or university faculty member who is delegated the responsibility to oversee students who are doing their directed (practice) teaching in the elementary and secondary schools. In business and industry supervision implies that one member of the firm has been hired to see to it that the other employees produce to the best of their ability.

Student teachers and employees in industry often refer to the supervisor as the *snoopervisor*. Unfortunately, many individuals charged with the responsibility of overseeing the work of others *earn* this label. Perhaps it is because of the implications inherent in the word *snoop*ervisor that many camp directors shy away from having an organized method of supervision of the counseling staff. This should not be. Supervision is one of the most important aspects of administrative responsibilities in summer camps.

To approach the subject from a more positive point of view, let us look to the actual definitions of the words supervise and supervision. According to Webster's New Collegiate Dictionary, to supervise means "a critical watching and directing (as of activities or a course of action)." The definition would imply that the role of the supervisor carries with it some authority. He must be able to oversee what is going on and must have the power to offer and give directions with the assurance that the one being supervised is obligated to effect a change where indicated.

What kind of a person should be chosen to be a supervisor? What traits must he possess if he is to supervise rather than snoopervise? The word *supervision* provides us with the clues. Actually the word is two words—*super* and *vision*. Examining these words individually, we find that they are defined as follows:

super   superior, above, over, more than, that surpasses all or most others of its kind

vision   something seen otherwise than by ordinary sight, unusual discernment or foresight

It would seem, then, that the person designated as a supervisor must have vision that is superior to those individuals he will be called upon to supervise. He must be able to look at a situation and *see* things that ordinary sight will not reveal. In addition to his background, training, personality, and genuine liking for people, the supervisor must have and wear a pair of special, invisible glasses that allow him to pierce through the obvious and arrive at the hidden factors that are operative in a situation.

Does popularity guarantee that the person will be a good supervisor? Not necessarily. He may not be popular with the group, but he must be well liked if individuals under him are to put forth extra effort to measure up.

Does superior knowledge make an individual a good supervisor? Not necessarily. Sometimes the smartest counselor is the least effective in human relations. But it is essential that he possess sound knowledge in the area of his supervision assignment.

Does a pleasing personality insure that the person will be a good supervisor? Not necessarily. It is true that he must be emotionally mature, objective in his judgment, patient, friendly, and able to relate easily with others, but he must be more than all that these delightful traits imply. He must possess knowledge, and he must inspire others to want to be better than they are.

How does supervision fit into the scheme of things during the summer at a resident camp? In many ways. Camp counselors need daily supervision in their counseling of children. Frequent staff meetings and formal and informal small group discussion periods that focus on understanding children provide opportunities for supervising the success counselors are having in meeting the needs of their campers. The director or a designated member of the staff must be highly competent in the skills necessary for this kind of supervision. Unit leaders sometimes assume responsibility for supervising the counseling techniques that individuals use. The question of whether unit leaders are always the best qualified for this kind of supervision should be raised, however. Often they are not.

As was pointed out in the preceding section, activity heads have the obligation to supervise the quality of the instruction each member of his staff is providing the campers. This means that counselors designated as heads of activities (such as waterfront, riding, archery, tennis, arts and crafts) must have a flexible teaching schedule that permits them freedom to visit classes that are in progress throughout the course of the day.

Even supervisors need supervision. From the top of the camp ladder to the bottom, an adequate system of supervision must be operative. The unit leader or activity head is responsible for the immediate supervision of counselors. The program director or assistant director or both supervise the unit leaders and activity heads. These two individuals are under the watchful eye of the director.

And what about the director? He also needs supervision. Who provides it? It depends on the structure of the camp. If, in private camping, the owner and director are two different people, the owner will certainly be concerned with the kind of job the director is doing. If the owner and director are the same person, a top administrative staff, perhaps the assistant director and program director, should be available as a source of guidance. In agency camping, the camp board supervises the director.

And who supervises the camp board? It should be someone representing the source of the greatest financial support of the agency. In some communities this source may be the United Fund board or the Community Chest. Another form of camp director supervision is provided by the Standards Committee visitation program of the ACA. In some states the State Department of Health exercises a measure of supervision of camp directors through its camp licensing regulations.

The supervisor cannot do an adequate job of supervision sitting at a desk. He must be in the field where the action is taking place. Activity heads must be able to observe their staff in teaching situations. Unit leaders must see counselors at work with campers in group living situations. Programming is more than paper and pencil work. Program directors and assistant directors must be able to observe the success of the program as it actually unfolds in day-to-day activities. Through consultations with the staff and the campers and on-the-spot inspections, the director can see the results of the administrative efforts of his staff and the counseling techniques of his counselors. In agency camps board members must make an effort to see what is going on during the course of "normal" days at camp, as well as on special events days.

One final thought on the subject of supervision in a camp setting seems appropriate. *Smothervision* is as bad, if not worse, than snoopervision. It is possible for the supervisor to be too solicitous, overly protective, or demanding. When the supervisor forgets what his role is and resorts to being the practitioner, the person being observed is unable to function in his assigned role. Human beings must be allowed to exercise judgment, make decisions, suffer frustrations, and have a failure or two along the way if they are to learn, grow, and mature as successful camp counselors. A good supervisor nurtures the freedom that allows individual initiative and maturation to blossom forth. He knows that his responsibility is to see to it that the job is done well, not to step in and do the work himself. Camp directors should become familiar with literature dealing with techniques of supervision.

They might find some of the sources to be of such value that they will develop a camp library and make resources available to camp personnel who carry the heaviest responsibility for supervision.

In summary nobody wants or needs *snoopervision* or *smothervision*, but everybody needs the guidance of someone who possesses vision that is super.

A camp director sent out post cards to the campers shortly after camp was over and asked the youngsters to write down what they had learned at camp and what had been important to them. One card came back with this honest evaluation on it: "I finally learned the difference between jam and jelly."

Are we kidding ourselves in camping? Do we really accomplish what the literature states is the wholesome outgrowth of a residential camp experience? Of course, we do. But, without an adequate system for evaluating our summer's operation, there may be a great deal of truth in the "jam and jelly" report.

What should be evaluated? Everything: the kitchen and its entire operation; the maintenance staff; the laundry facilities and procedures; activity areas and equipment; the program; all policies, rules, and regulations; the campers; the counselors; the administrative staff; and anything else that pertains to the functioning of the camp operation. Evaluations should be in written form. Discussion sessions are of great value, but the conclusions in the form of recommendations should be written down for reconsideration in the fall and spring prior to the opening of the next camp season. The individuals directly responsible for the kitchen, maintenance, the laundry, and the program should make a final written report that goes beyond what is asked for on the usual inventory sheet. What went well? Where were the problem areas? What would make the operation run more smoothly next summer? Counselors responsible for overseeing an activity area should make the final written report after they have given the staff an opportunity to make suggestions. Often the program director would benefit from having a meeting with all heads of activities to evaluate the overall program. What went well? Where were there hitches? What should be revised for next summer? What should be changed completely or dropped from the program? Was the staff adequate for the jobs that needed to be done? Were they competent? Were there enough?

Counselors as well as campers should have an opportunity to discuss the camp policies, rules, and regulations and to make recommendations for improvement. This could be done through cabin group discussions and followed up with a written report from each group. Which rules caused the most disgruntlement? Were there some that seemed inappropriate? Were the rules clearly understood? The counselor's evaluation should be kept separate from the campers' when put in written form. In other words the cabin counselor should evaluate the campers evaluation. Both should be turned in, whether the counselor agrees with the campers or not.

The counselor's evaluation of each individual camper is of little value if it is not shared with the camper. Counselors should be informed during precamp of the type of evaluation they will be expected to make on their campers throughout the camp session. Counselors should likewise be evaluated. This can be done in many ways. Heads of activities should indicate the success or lack of success the counselor experienced as a teacher. What were his strong points? What were his weak points? Should he be given an opportunity to come back next summer in the same job assignment? Unit leaders should be able to evaluate the kind of job the counselor did in his group living assignments. If the structure of the camp does not provide for unit leaders, someone in the camp should be able to make such an evaluation or else the obligation to provide adequate supervision is not being met. The type of evaluation made on the counselor should be in line with the application blank and the recommendation sheets used by the camp. A sample of one type of written counselor evaluation form is included as an example of how such a form could be constructed. Directors are welcome to use the form just as it is or to modify it in any way that might be appropriate to their particular camp.

Thus far we have been concerned with final evaluations. For evaluations to be meaningful, however, they should be ongoing. The first evaluation should be done during precamp and should concern the precamp session. It should be in written form. Throughout the camp session, whether it is five days or eight weeks, there should be an alertness on the part of the entire camp family to how things are going. If a change seems to be necessary or beneficial, and if it is possible to institute the change during the course of a session, then there should be freedom to make such a change. Camps that operate several short sessions during the course of the summer have an excellent opportunity to evaluate the entire operation at the close of each session and make the necessary modifications for a more successful session that is to follow. Such evaluations take time, but their importance is paramount. It is just plain foolishness to repeat the same mistakes over and over. Directors of long-session camps must make extra effort to have ongoing evaluations because it is so easy to just slide along doing the same old thing in the same old way when everything seems to be going well. There is always room for improvement.

If a counselor is not doing his job particularly well, he should know it early enough to be given an opportunity to demonstrate that he can do better. By the same token, a camper should know where he stands so that he will have time to show improvement before the final report is filled out.

There is merit in putting a few thoughts down on paper immediately after the camp season ends. Final evaluations are often done when the haste and pressures of the final week prevent thinking clearly or objectively. A short-answer post card evaluation could be sent to campers, parents, and counselors.

This makes lots of extra reading for the poor, tired director, you say. Yes, it does. But a little extra midnight oil burned during December, January, and February might make it possible for the director to have more restful days and nights during the camp session the following summer.

Suggested readings

Brightbill, C. K. *Man and Leisure.* Englewood Cliffs, N. J.: Prentice-Hall, Inc., 1961.
Frostic, G. *A Walk With Me.* Michigan: Gwen Frostic, 1958.
Frostic, G. *These Things Are Ours.* Michigan: Gwen Frostic, 1960.
Gardner, J. W. *Excellence.* New York: Harper & Row, Publishers, 1961.
Grahame, K. *The Wind in the Willows.* New York: The Heritage Press, 1940.
White, E. B. *Charlotte's Web.* New York: Harper & Row, Publishers, 1952.

part III

counseling and guidance

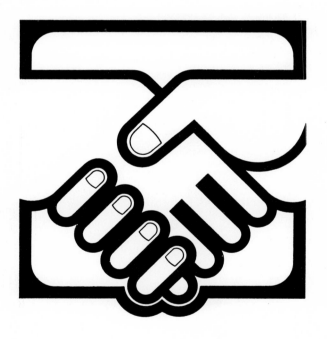

The Counselor

Develop a love for people.

Personal qualifications and characteristics

Many studies have been conducted to determine how to predict who will be successful as a camp counselor. Personality tests, attitude measurements, and interest inventories, along with rating scales of all sorts, have all been employed—to no avail. No screening device has been able to conclusively predict successful camp counselors. *Having* certain personal traits and characteristics is not enough—the success of a counselor depends upon how he *uses* these qualities in the camp setting.

Positive characteristics

Camp directors are in agreement that certain personal characteristics are important to a counselor's chances of being successful (Schmitt, 1965). These characteristics are listed in the order of their importance in the following exercise:

To do

Write a brief description of what you understand these characteristics to mean:
1. Exhibits emotional maturity
2. Moral character and integrity
3. Considers the camper's needs first
4. Understands needs of campers
5. Liking for children
6. Ability to adjust
7. Works easily with others
8. Willingness to learn
9. Contributes to objectives of the camp
10. Shows good health and vitality
11. Enjoys the out-of-doors
12. Skills for specific responsibilities

To do

1. Why do you think "Skills for specific responsibilities" is ranked at the bottom of the list?

2. Why do you think emotional maturity is ranked at the top of the list?

Negative characteristics

Characteristics deemed detrimental to success as a counselor (not necessarily in order of priority) are:

28

1. Immaturity
2. Not having a liking for or understanding children
3. Putting personal pleasure first
4. Inability to work with others
5. Lack of ability to adjust to camp environment
6. Unwillingness to learn
7. Inability to take directions and constructive criticism
8. Laziness
9. Inability to establish and maintain proper camper-counselor relationships
10. Lack of sense of humor
11. Failure to get enough rest, which results in poor physical and mental health
12. Giving more attention to camp staff than to campers
13. Failure to maintain proper atmosphere for discipline
14. Showing partiality
15. Impatience with campers

Self-evaluation

You're only young once, but you can be immature indefinitely.

Emotional maturity is essential to success as a counselor, and immaturity is deemed detrimental to success.

To do

Take stock of yourself by filling out the Emotional Maturity Rating Sheet (p. 29) developed by Mitchell and Crawford. Use a pencil. Four weeks from now, check to see if you would revise any of your answers.

Desirable skill qualifications

General

All counselors should have *some knowledge* in the following areas:
1. Growth and development characteristics of the age group with which he is working
2. Individual and group guidance and counseling
3. Waterfront activities
4. Popular recreational land sports and games
5. Nature lore and its related activities
6. Outdoor cooking skills
7. Campfires
8. Storytelling and dramatics
9. Group singing
10. First aid
11. Safety
12. Sanitation

Specific

Many camps hire specialists in the areas indicated above, but cabin counselors and general counselors are expected to be tolerant of *all* phases of the program. If preferences or prejudices toward certain activities exist, the counselor should not let them negatively influence the campers' enthusiasm for the program. Specific skill areas in which specialization may be an asset when seeking employment as a camp counselor are arts and crafts, na-

SELF EVALUATION RATING SCALE	Poor 1	Below Average 2	Average 3	Above Average 4	Superior 5
1. Can you accept criticism without undue anger or hurt, acting upon it if justified, disregarding it if not?					
2. Are you tolerant of others and willing to overlook their faults?					
3. Do you feel genuinely happy at the success of others and sincerely congratulate them?					
4. Do you refrain from listening to and repeating undue gossip about others?					
5. Do you converse about other things and persons? Test it by checking your conversation to see how frequently you use "I".					
6. Are you altruistic, often putting the welfare and happiness of others above your own?					
7. Do you refrain from emotional outbursts of anger, tears, etc.?					
8. Do you face disagreeable duties promptly and without trying to escape by playing sick or making excuses?					
9. Can you stay away from home a month or more without undue homesickness?					
10. Can you weigh facts and make decisions promptly, then abide by your decisions?					
11. Are you willing to postpone things you want to do now in favor of greater benefits or pleasure later?					
12. Are you usually on good terms with your family and associates?					
13. When things go wrong, can you objectively determine the cause and remedy it without alibiing for yourself and blaming it on other people or things?					
14. When disagreeing with another, can you discuss it calmly and usually work out a mutually satisfactory agreement without hard feelings?					
15. Can you enter into informal social events of many types wholeheartedly?					
16. Do you really enjoy doing little things for others, even though you know they will likely go unknown and unappreciated?					
17. Do you dress neatly and modestly without tendency to gaudiness or overdress?					
18. Can you dismiss past sins and mistakes that can't be remedied now without dwelling on them?					
19. Can you make decisions regarding others objectively, disregarding your personal dislike or resentment of them?					
20. As a leader, do you work democratically without dictating or forcing your will on others?					
21. Are you loyal to your friends, minimizing or not mentioning their faults to others?					
22. Are you free from "touchiness," so that others do not have to handle you with kid gloves?					
23. Do you act according to your honest convictions regardless of what others may think or say about it?					
24. Do you have a kindly feeling toward most people, a deep affection for some, and no unhealthy attachments to any?					
25. Do you feel that you usually get about what you deserve? Are you free from a feeling that others "have it in for" you?					

ture lore and conservation, trips, waterfront (swimming, diving, and small craft), special land sports (tennis, riding, rifle, golf, and so on), music, dramatics, and writing and journalism.

To do

1. Put one check by the general areas you already know something about.
2. Put two checks by the areas in which you are already a specialist.
3. Put an asterisk by the area(s) in which you would like to become a specialist.

Responsibilities

I am only one, but still I am one.
I cannot do everything, yet I can do something.
And since I cannot do everything
I shall not refuse to do something I can do.
                                    Anonymous

Responsibilities to self

Make of yourself what you want others to think you are.

Responsibilities to the director

1. Putting forth your best self
2. Loyalty
3. Working toward the accomplishment of the camp's goals
4. Observing all rules, including health and safety (the spirit of the rules as well as the letter)
5. Promptness at all meetings, with written reports, and so on
6. Efficient, capable handling of duties
7. Good conduct in and out of camp
8. No requests for special favors and privileges
9. Cooperation and enthusiasm
10. Your best efforts
11. Use of the referral system when additional help is needed

To do

List others:

Responsibilities to the campers

1. Putting forth your best self. Sometimes a child can help you be better than you are.
2. Providing a "star" for the camper to reach for. Other campers are his playmates, *you* are his inspiration.
3. Impartiality. Anyone can like the cute, friendly camper, but *you* are responsible for *all* of the campers.
4. Being a partner in upholding traditions, ideals, and policies of camp.
5. Respecting the individuality of each camper and his right to his point of view.

6. Understanding the physical, mental, emotional, and social characteristics of the children and of their specific environmental backgrounds.
7. Being an enthusiastic supporter of the campers' activities.
8. Making the cabin or tent a *home* instead of a house.

To do

List others:

Responsibilities to other counselors

1. Consideration of others' privacy, and of their equipment, property, and time.
2. Friendliness, tact, patience, and loyalty to *each* counselor.
3. Appreciation of the contributions that each counselor makes to the total camp program. Everyone's role is important—*there are no small jobs* at camp.
4. No rumor spreading regarding others.
5. No unnecessary discussion of camp rules or policies among one another without first discussing them with the director.
6. Cooperation and assistance in all group efforts.
7. Open-mindedness.
8. Asking no favors and not expecting to be waited on by anyone.

To do

List others:

Responsibilities to parents

1. Be the best parent substitute possible.
2. Be truthful, but tactful, in all reports and conversations.
3. Notify immediately in case of sickness or accident, but have it cleared through the director.
4. Make sure that child writes home at least once a week.

To do

List others:

To do

In the space below, give two examples of how you have discharged your responsibilities to the director, the campers, the other counselors, and the parents.

Cite five examples of how a counselor can be a good public relations ambassador for the camp.

DUTIES OF A COUNSELOR*

1. Arise daily with campers, except on day off, and report to flag raising with cabinmates by 7:05 AM.
2. Supervise completion of cabin duty assignments, (caper chart, and so on) and see that these are executed satisfactorily.
3. See that your campers are neat and clean at meals, classes, and programs.
4. Be a hostess in the dining room at each meal except for specified meals and day off. With honor camper hostesses, counselors may be relieved of noon meal supervision.
5. Maintain cabin discipline with consistency, fairness, cheerfulness, and enthusiasm.
6. Be responsible for quiet in the cabin at rest hour, after taps, and also before reveille.
7. Encourage campers in your cabin to eat well-balanced meals and to use acceptable table manners.
8. Accompany campers to programs.
9. Be able to teach at least one activity well.
10. Take office duty when assigned.
11. Be an example, an inspiration, and an aid to the CIT assigned to you and give her opportunities for leadership development within the cabin structure.
12. Be responsible for the health, safety, and happiness of each member of the cabin group, and seek aid from proper sources when the need arises (doctor, nurse, and camp director).
13. Get away from camp and refresh yourself on your 24-hour leave and during your evenings off after taps.
14. Provide guidance to each camper in the use of free time.
15. Be cordial, hospitable, and friendly to parents visiting camp.
16. Be able to discuss intelligently the strengths and weaknesses of each camper in the cabin with the director and parents.
17. Write an evaluation of each camper to the parents at the end of the fourth and seventh weeks.
18. Be loyal to the director and abide by the statements in your contract.

---

*From an actual situation.

Cite five examples of behavior that would be appropriate at school that would not be appropriate in your role as a camp counselor. Why?

Applying for a camp counseling position

The following are sources of information on camps:

1. Annual Camp Directory, published by the American Camping Association, Bradford Woods, Martinsville, Indiana 46151. This directory includes all of the camps in the United States that are members of ACA.
2. State camping associations. Write to ACA headquarters at Bradford Woods to secure names of presidents of state camping associations. The presidents can send you state directories.
3. Placement service bureaus in colleges and universities.
4. Departments of recreation and departments of physical education in colleges and universities.
5. City and county social and welfare agencies.
6. Youth serving organizations—Boy Scouts, Girl Scouts, Campfire Girls, Boys Club of America, Girls Club of America, YMCA, YWCA, YMHA, YWHA, CYO, and so on.
7. The Camping Magazine, published by ACA.
8. Nationally distributed magazines that have camping sections, for example, Redbook, National Observer.

To consider alternative camps objectively, find out the location, dates of the camping season, its objectives, aims and philosophy, its program and emphasis, the background, age, sex, and number of campers, the background and number of staff members, the percentage of staff who return for the second and third years, the terrain and layout of the camp, and the sponsorship or ownership of the camp (private or agency).

Before signing the contract determine whether you are in agreement with the camp's philosophy and general policies; the salary; the exact dates of the commitment; specific policies regarding time off, smoking, and so on that will directly affect your behavior; insurance coverage; sick benefits; and the specific responsibilities inherent in the position.

When writing a letter of inquiry, remember it is a business letter and use formal stationary. (Typing paper is better than floral, scented stationary); type the letter and check for typographical errors; use correct grammar and punctuation and if necessary, get a competent "editor" to check it for you; make the letter brief but include your best selling points and try to arouse the director's interest to the point that he will follow up on you as a good prospect. If you are a college student, include your college classification, major, age, area of special preparation (W.S.I., riding, dramatics, campcrafter, and so on) and number of years previous camping experience and related experiences. If you have had a CIT or camp leadership course, indicate where and when. Ask if any positions will be available on the staff for the coming summer and indicate that you would like to be considered in the event there is an opening. Once communication has been established between you and the director, find out more about the camp and the director can find out more about you. The letter of inquiry *just begins* the communication process. It will give the director his first impression of you, and, since first impressions are sometimes lasting ones, put your best self forward.

Fill out the application blank accurately and neatly. Be *truthful*. The director does not expect you to be an expert in all program areas but will expect you to be able to do what you say you can do.

Before giving a person's name as a reference, ask his permission. If the person does not wish to serve as a reference and does not return the recommendation sheet to the director, the director may wonder about your suitability for the job. Give names of adults who can best vouch for your character, emotional maturity, and ability to work with others. Good prospects for references are previous employers, supervisors where you have done volunteer work, faculty advisers, dormitory directors, and teachers. Unless you are stuck for names, do not give your minister, priest, or rabbi as a reference. Everybody always expects him to give a good recommendation. We suggest that you *not* state the salary you desire, even if the question is asked on the application blank. It is the responsibility of the director to make an offer first. In the blank space on the application blank (or in conversation with the director) the answer should be, "Depends upon the responsibilities inherent in the position for which I am hired."

It is desirable to arrange a personal interview. Prior to the interview, formulate definite reasons why you want to be a camp counselor and why you are interested in a position at that specific camp. If you have had a previous counseling position, be prepared to explain why you do not wish to return to that camp.

The director will use the opportunity to become acquainted with you and with your qualifications. It is, of course, important to be well groomed. Hair should be clean and neat; clean shave or groomed beard, or fresh make-up; teeth brushed; sweet breath; deodorant; clean finger nails; clean shirt or blouse; clothes pressed; shoes shined. If you are carelessly groomed, the director may conclude that you are a careless person and that you cannot function without close supervision.

You will be judged not only by what you say but by how you say it, so use good English. Slang may be appropriate with your peers but the director wants to know if you can carry on a conversation with campers' parents.

Answer questions truthfully and directly.

The interview also provides you with an opportunity to get acquainted with the director and the camp. It will be a good time to find out pertinent details about the camp that were discussed previously.

It is important to remember that you are not *asking* for a job. You are aggressively *selling* your services.

The terms of employment may be in the form of a printed contract or an informal letter. The purpose of the agreement is to state mutual obligations and to assure each party (you and the director) that the other understands them. Contracts should include (1) names of contracting parties; (2) the salary to be paid and arrangements for paying (every two weeks, middle and end of the season, or end of the season); (3) deductions from salary (social security, taxes, and so on); (4) arrangements for room and board; (5) arrangements for transportation costs to and from camp when appropriate; (6) length of obligation, with stated time of arrival and departure; (7) length and interval of time off; (8) provisions for medical treatment, liability insurance, and emergency leave; (9) duties and responsibilities of position; (10) provisions for terminating contract; (11) date and signature of counselor and director; and (12) a copy of the signed contract for each party.

If a major event that you wish to attend will occur during the camp season and you know about it prior to signing the contract, ask the director if it would be possible for you to be away from camp on those specific days. It may be possible for you to be gone on those dates without a real inconvenience to the camp, or the director may feel that you can not be spared. Remember, if you sign the contract without prior arrangements, the director is under no obligation to permit you to leave camp for weddings, reunions, college placement tests, and so on.

To do

1. Write a letter of inquiry.
2. Fill out the application blanks to the best of your ability.
3. Study the recommendation sheets to see how persons listed as references are asked to vouch for you.
4. Study the sample contracts. Do they contain the items discussed under terms of employment?

Understanding the individual

Console, understand, love.

In a counselor's efforts to understand children and others, he should keep in mind the old adage "Confused bewilderment of the centipede who was quite happy until a frog in fun said, 'Pray, which leg come after which?' This raised his mind to such a pitch he lay distracted in the ditch considering how to run." However, just because there are so many dimensions to that phenomenon in nature—man—we should not become so confused and bewildered that we make no effort to understand him as an individual.

As an individual, the camper should be accorded the same considerations the adult wants for himself. These considerations include understanding, patience, kindness, forgiveness, and perhaps most important of all—a second chance. The following is a discussion of how camp counselors can show such consideration to their campers.

Understanding

One can hardly exaggerate the value of understanding others. How often each of us has said, "If he would just understand my point of view," or "She isn't a very understanding person." But what exactly are we asking for when we want others to understand us?

Understanding can be viewed from two angles—appreciation and knowledge. It first requires an appreciation, or awareness, of each individual's worth as a human being. It is a recognition of the fact that each individual exists for some unique purpose. Such an appreciation creates a relationship between human beings that elevates even the lowliest among us to a position of dignity. To be sure, this implies that no matter how badly a camper has behaved, the counselor is aware that within that child there is goodness or the potential for goodness and that it is the counselor's obligation to seek and bring out this quality in the camper. Camping literature is replete with statements regarding the spiritual values that can be derived from camping. Those of us in camping can translate the spiritual values that are expounded at campfires into our daily living. We can begin by understanding and appreciating each camper's worth as a human being.

Understanding also requires knowledge. For camp counselors this means a knowledge of child growth and development. Counselors should know the answers to such questions as, What causes temper tantrums?, What fears are normal for nine-year-olds?, or Is it normal for a twelve-year-old to be smitten with hero worship?

Text continued on p. 55.

CAMP STAFF APPLICATION

Instructions: Type or print clearly.   Return to: Camp Administrator
             Enclose a recent photo.   Circle T Girl Scout Council
                                            3015 West Fifth St.
                                            Fort Worth, Texas 76107

Name | Telephone no. | Social security no.

Present address | Registered member of G.S.U.S.A.
☐ yes   ☐ no
If yes, state position:

Permanent address | Dates available for camp employment
From _____
To _____

| Date of birth | Height | Weight | Marital status ☐ single ☐ married ☐ other | Present occupation |

Position desired (check):

☐ Unit leader   ☐ Waterfront director   ☐ Business manager
☐ Unit assistant   ☐ Waterfront assistant   ☐ Health supervisor (nurse)
☐ Counselor-in-training ☐ Small craft director   ☐ Pack-out coordinator
    unit leader   ☐ Small craft assistant   ☐ Riding counselor

Name and address of school/college attended	Dates	Degree and/or major

Courses taken in camp training or leadership	Agency	Place	Dates

Camp positions held (list most recent first)	Employer name and address	Director or supervisor Name and address	Dates

Titles of other positions held	Employer name and address	Director or supervisor	Dates

Continued.

CAMP STAFF APPLICATION—cont'd

Check areas in which you have   (1) interest   (2) experience   (3) teaching knowledge:

1 2 3		1 2 3		1 2 3 Waterfront:	
☐☐☐	Archery	☐☐☐	Hand arts	☐☐☐	Canoeing
☐☐☐	Campcraft	☐☐☐	Horseback riding	☐☐☐	Rowing
☐☐☐	Dramatics	☐☐☐	Nature and conservation	☐☐☐	Sailing
☐☐☐	First aid	☐☐☐	Photography	☐☐☐	Swimming
☐☐☐	Folk dancing	☐☐☐	Primitive camping		
☐☐☐	Games—sports	☐☐☐	Song leading		

Experience as a camper (✔)

☐ Day camping   ☐ Primitive encampment   ☐ Roundup
☐ Troop camping   ☐ Inter-council encampment   ☐ International encampment
☐ Established camping   All-states encampment   Other (explain)

Experience with Girl Scout troops

Capacity _____ Age group _____
Describe briefly:

Have you completed   Counselor-in-training? ☐ yes   Leader-in-training? ☐ yes

Experience with other age groups (✔)   Circle the group you prefer

☐ 7-8 yrs.   ☐ 9-11 yrs.   ☐ 12-14 yrs.   ☐ 15-17 yrs.

Other skills or experience:

Certified life saver   ☐   Check classification and year.
                                        ☐ Junior 19 __   ☐ Senior 19 __

Waterfront instructor ☐   Check source of training and year.
                                        ☐ Red Cross   ☐ YMCA   ☐ Boy Scouts
                                        19 __   19 __   19 __

Small craft instructor ☐   Check course and year.
   (Red Cross)   ☐ Rowing   ☐ Canoeing   ☐ Sailing
                                        19 __   19 __   19 __

American Camping
   Association courses   ☐ Campcrafter   ☐ Advanced campcrafter

Explain briefly why you are interested in a camp job and what you consider your main qualifications for the job.

List three persons, not related to you, who have definite knowledge of your qualifications for the position for which you are applying. College students should enter the name of a faculty adviser or dean of students in addition to references indicated on the other side.

Name	Address	Position

I understand that the presentation of a certificate of a satisfactory physical examination is a prerequisite to appointment.

_____   _____
Signature   Date

CIRCLE T GIRL SCOUT COUNCIL, INC.
3015 West Fifth Street
Fort Worth, Texas 76107

To whom it may concern

From: Director of Camping Services

_____ has given your name as a reference in applying for a camp position at one of the Circle T camps. Resident camping is a 24-hour-a-day living situation; therefore it is important that counselors and others on the staff enjoy and understand children, work well with other adults, and have a real love of outdoor living. The task of selecting the right staff for such an important position as summer camp leadership is difficult, and I would appreciate your analyzing as carefully as possible the above applicant. Your statement will be considered confidential.

As further action depends on your response, your prompt attention to this matter will be appreciated. Thank you for your consideration.

1. How long and in what capacity have you known applicant?_____

2. In your opinion is applicant mature enough to:
   a. be responsible for children in a camp setting?   ____yes ____no
   b. guide girls in a program of simple democratic living?   ____yes ____no
   c. get along with co-workers under close living conditions? ____yes ____no
   d. assume responsibility for carrying out delegated duties? ____yes ____no
   e. accept on-going guidance and supervision?   ____yes ____no

   Comments _____

3. Do you know of any religious, cultural, or racial prejudice applicant might have that would limit her ability to work with all children and staff?   ____yes ____no

   Comments _____

4. Please comment on applicant's personal appearance _____

5. In your opinion do you think the applicant is physically able to enjoy a summer of active outdoor living? ____yes ____no

   Comments _____

Continued.

6. Please check the statements which best describe this applicant.

__Almost always seems happy

__Gets along well with people of all types

__Accepts suggestions and corrections graciously

__Seems to have self-confidence

__Is adaptable to new situations

__Is tolerant of other's ideas and desires

__Takes initiative

__Has a genuine interest in people

__Is often moody and depressed

__Gets angry easily, loses temper

__Feels that supervisors are unduly critical

__Seems to lack self-confidence

__Finds change difficult

__Tends to be dictatorial

__Seems to enjoy dissension

__Seems to be self-centered

__Does not make a good first impression but wears well

7. Is the applicant capable of motivating children and stimulating their interest?

____ yes ____ no   Comments _____

_____

8. Is applicant's character and attitudes such that her influence on young girls would be desirable?   ____ yes ____ no

Comments _____

_____

9. How would you rate applicant as a potential camp counselor?

_____ Exceptionally strong   _____ Average

_____ Above average   _____ Below average

10. Please make any additional comments you think might be helpful to us in determining whether this applicant has the qualifications to work with young girls.

_____

_____

_____

_____

Date _____   Signature _____

Position _____

CONTRACT AGREEMENT
BETWEEN
CIRCLE T GIRL SCOUT COUNCIL

Name _____ Address _____ Phone _____

_____
Permanent address

FOR CAMP TIMBERLAKE   OR   STEVENS RANCH ON THE BRAZOS

Who agrees to comply with camp requirements and to fulfill the duties and responsi-

bilities of _____ for the period beginning _____

and ending _____. This includes the precamp conference.

1. It is agreed that the person named will receive the following:
   a. Board and room while at camp
   b. Precamp training
   c. Salary _____
   d. Social security coverage
   e. Workmen's compensation and accident and sickness coverage
2. It is agreed that free time will be given as follows:
   One 24-hour period during each 2-week session.
   One 24-hour period between sessions.
3. In the event of cancellation on the part of either the Circle T Girl Scout Council or the camp staff member, payment of salary will be prorated to the date the cancellation becomes effective.
4. All federal and state tax requirements including federal withholding tax regulations will apply.
5. It is agreed that the individual employed will present a statement of satisfactory physical condition by a licensed physician in accordance with Girl Scout camp standards.
6. It is understood that the employing group cannot be responsible for personal items or valuables.

TO BE NOTIFIED IN CASE OF EMERGENCY:

Name _____ Address _____ Phone _____

Signed _____ Date _____
            Camp Staff Member

_____ Date _____
Camp Director

_____ Date _____
Director of Camping Services

Houston YMCA Camps

HOUSTON YMCA BOYS CAMP

WIMBERLEY, TEXAS

"To enlist people in a worldwide fellowship, to aid them in developing Christian personalities, and to instill in them a desire for building a Christian society by maintaining such activities and services as contribute to their spiritual, mental, physical, and social growth."

If you are interested in applying for a position on the camp staff, please provide the information requested herein, and return this application.

Name _____ Age _____

Birthplace _____ Date _____, 19 _____

School or business Address _____
    City _____ State _____ Phone _____

Permanent home address _____
    City _____ State _____ Phone _____

Height __'__" Weight _____ Married? _____ Children _____

Physical defects, if any _____

Church membership _____ Active? _____

Occupation, position _____

Father's name and occupation _____
Mother's name and occupation _____

ATTACH PHOTOGRAPH HERE

(Snapshot will do)

Armed Service status _____
    (If veteran, give branch, length of service, rank, any foreign duty, date of discharge)

Of what social, professional, political, or other organizations, clubs, or societies are you a member? _____

Are you a member of a union? _____ If yes, give name: _____

Licenses and certificates held _____ Social Security Card No. _____

Previously employed by YMCA? _____ Position held and date _____

What position are you applying for? _____ Who referred you to us? _____

A Camp leader's responsibility in camp is serious and exacting. His rewards are found largely in the satisfaction of a job well done and in the personal growth and development that goes with it. Your signature below indicates your sympathy with the purpose stated above and your willingness to give your best efforts and ability in achieving it.

Date _____ Signature _____

Continued.

ADDITIONAL   INFORMATION

PLEASE SUMMARIZE YOUR EDUCATIONAL HISTORY IN THE CHART BELOW:

High School or College Attended	Present Classification or Degree Received	Major Subjects	Average Grade
1. _____	_____	_____	_____
2. _____	_____	_____	_____
3. _____	_____	_____	_____
4. _____	_____	_____	_____

Circle final year spent in school: High School 1 2 3 4   College 1 2 3 4   Graduate 1 2 3 4

If not in college, do you expect to go? _____ When and Where? _____

What are, or were, your chief college or high school interests? _____

In what college or high school organizations are, or were, you active? Give name and positions held: _____
_____

Give names and authors of two or three books you have read recently which deal with psychology, sociology, religion, or education _____
_____

What contribution did they make to your thinking? Comment _____
_____

What courses of study have you had that could apply to a camp experience? _____
_____

What actual experience have you had as a leader in camp? _____   When and where? Be specific _____
_____
_____

What special duties did you have? _____

Have you had experience in leading other groups during the year? _____

What kinds of groups? _____
What kinds of activities? _____

Give details of your other qualifications for camp leadership_____
_____
_____

What are some of your hobbies? _____

Do you have YMCA, Red Cross, or Scout Certificates in Life Saving? _____ If so, state highest certificate attained, date earned, expiration date: _____
(If not a Senior Life Saver, indicate swimming ability)

What age group of campers do you prefer to work with? _____

Will you be available from _____ , 19 __ to _____ , 19 __ ?

Yes _____   No _____

44

ACTIVITY CHECK LIST

Please check the degree of your participation, interest, and skill and knowledge in each of the activities listed below:

PARTICIPATION			ACTIVITIES	INTEREST			SKILL OR KNOWLEDGE		
Much	Some	Never		Like	Indifferent	Dislike	Much	Some	None
___	___	___	Arts and Crafts	___	___	___	___	___	___
___	___	___	Beadwork	___	___	___	___	___	___
___	___	___	Bow & Arrows	___	___	___	___	___	___
___	___	___	Carpentry	___	___	___	___	___	___
___	___	___	Cartooning	___	___	___	___	___	___
___	___	___	Drawing, Painting	___	___	___	___	___	___
___	___	___	Leatherwork	___	___	___	___	___	___
___	___	___	Photography	___	___	___	___	___	___
___	___	___	Archery	___	___	___	___	___	___
___	___	___	Boating	___	___	___	___	___	___
___	___	___	Camp Bugler	___	___	___	___	___	___
___	___	___	Campfire Programs	___	___	___	___	___	___
___	___	___	Canoe Trips	___	___	___	___	___	___
___	___	___	Conducting Worship	___	___	___	___	___	___
___	___	___	Dramatics & plays	___	___	___	___	___	___
___	___	___	Direct Camp Band	___	___	___	___	___	___
___	___	___	Edit Camp Paper	___	___	___	___	___	___
___	___	___	Fishing	___	___	___	___	___	___
___	___	___	Health & First-Aid	___	___	___	___	___	___
___	___	___	Hikes & Over-nights	___	___	___	___	___	___
___	___	___	Horseback Riding	___	___	___	___	___	___
___	___	___	Indian Lore	___	___	___	___	___	___
___	___	___	Lead Group Singing	___	___	___	___	___	___
___	___	___	Lead Discussions	___	___	___	___	___	___
___	___	___	Minstrels & Circus	___	___	___	___	___	___
___	___	___	Nature Study	___	___	___	___	___	___
___	___	___	Animals, birds, fish	___	___	___	___	___	___
___	___	___	Insects, reptiles	___	___	___	___	___	___
___	___	___	Trees and rocks	___	___	___	___	___	___
___	___	___	Stars and planets	___	___	___	___	___	___
___	___	___	Weather	___	___	___	___	___	___
___	___	___	Outdoor Cooking	___	___	___	___	___	___
___	___	___	Radio & Signaling	___	___	___	___	___	___
___	___	___	Rifle Shooting	___	___	___	___	___	___
___	___	___	Singing, quartette	___	___	___	___	___	___
___	___	___	Sports	___	___	___	___	___	___
___	___	___	Softball	___	___	___	___	___	___
___	___	___	Basketball	___	___	___	___	___	___
___	___	___	Football	___	___	___	___	___	___
___	___	___	Golf	___	___	___	___	___	___
___	___	___	Swimming	___	___	___	___	___	___
___	___	___	Tennis	___	___	___	___	___	___
___	___	___	Track & Field	___	___	___	___	___	___
___	___	___	Volleyball	___	___	___	___	___	___
___	___	___	Story Telling	___	___	___	___	___	___
___	___	___	Typewriting	___	___	___	___	___	___

Do you play a musical instrument? _____ Will you bring it? _____ Operate movie projector? _____

    What? _____

Continued.

PLEASE ANSWER THE FOLLOWING QUESTIONS

What do you consider to be the function of a YMCA Camp?

What results would you want to achieve in the behavior of campers under your leadership?

When a YMCA Camp is spoken of in terms of an agency for the development of character and personality, what does this mean to you?

If you were in charge of a cabin group and asked to put on a stunt at the campfire tomorrow night, what would you do in preparation?

If some T-shirts belonging to a camper in your cabin were missing and you suspected a certain camper had them, what would you do?

If another leader spent a lot of time "griping" about camp program and management when in your company, what would you do?

LIST BELOW THREE PEOPLE WHO KNOW YOU AND CAN GIVE US A DEFINITE STATEMENT AS TO YOUR CHARACTER, ABILITY AND WORK HABITS:

NAME	Address	City	State	POSITION	HOW LONG KNOWN
Teacher:					
1.					
Minister:					
2.					
Employer:					
3.					

••••••••••••••••••••••••••••••••••••• PLEASE DO NOT WRITE BELOW THIS LINE •••••••••••••••••••••••••••••••••••••

Interviewed by _____ Date _____ , 19 ____   References written _____ 19 ____

Application received (Date) _____ , 19 ____   Replies received:

Contract Mailed _____ , 19 ____   1. _____ 19 ____
                                                   2. _____ 19 ____
                                                   3. _____ 19 ____
Contract Received _____ , 19 ____

CAMP OFFICE
1600 LOUISIANA, HOUSTON 2, TEXAS

PHONE: CA 4-9501

HOUSTON YMCA BOYS' CAMP

ATTITUDE RATING FORM

Dear _____

_____ has applied for the position of

_____ on our YMCA Boys' Summer Camp Staff.

Please rate him on the scale below in relation to this responsible position of leadership to boys from 8 to 15 years of age. Place a check mark on the scale only where
you are sure of your knowledge of him in that area.

1. SOCIAL ACCEPTANCE
                Highly Sociable   Average Sociability   Poor

2. RESPONSIBILITY

Does he complete the job
using his own initiative
or does he need to be told   Very Responsible   Average   Poor
everything to be done.

3. ALL-AROUND EXEMPLIFICATION
    OF GENUINE CHRISTIAN CHARACTER

    Consistently Exemplified   Conforms to   Inconsistent
      Highest Standard   Unusual Standard

4. COOPERATIVE ATTITUDE
              Very   Average   Poor

5. INDUSTRY
Does he keep busy
or is he lazy?

6. ANY PERSONAL REMARKS YOU WISH TO MAKE:

_____

_____

_____

_____

THIS INFORMATION IS CONFIDENTIAL

PLEASE MAIL IN THE ENCLOSED ENVELOPE AT YOUR EARLIEST CONVENIENCE. THANK YOU!

YMCA OF THE GREATER HOUSTON AREA, TEXAS

HOUSTON YMCA BOYS' CAMP

PERSONNEL CONTRACT

Name _____ Date _____

Position and Job Analysis:_____

_____

_____

_____

_____

_____

_____

_____

_____

Amount of Salary $_____(per week) $_____(per season)_____

Duration of Employment_____

I have read the GENERAL AGREEMENT and agree to abide by its stipulations.

I understand that the Camp Director has the right to terminate this contract at
any time, with salary paid to date of termination, if he believes my conduct
and attitude detrimental to the best interests of the camp. I understand that
all staff agreements may be terminated if the camp is closed by medical or civil
authority, or by action of the Metropolitan YMCA Board of Directors.

_____   _____

   Date   Signature of Employee

                                   _____

                                   Signature of Camp Director

                Sign and return one copy to:
                      YMCA CAMP OFFICE
                      1600 Louisiana
                   Houston, Texas 77002

49

```
KANAKUK KAMP            STAFF APPLICATION        KANAKOMO KAMP
   FOR BOYS                                          FOR GIRLS

                                         ┌─────────────────┐
Return to:  Kanakuk-Kanakomo Kamps, Inc. │      YOUR       │
            Lakeshore Drive              │    PICTURE      │
            Branson, Missouri    65616   │     HERE        │
                                         │   (Required!)   │
                                         └─────────────────┘

Name: (Mr., Mrs., Miss)_____
                        (Please print last name first)

Your home address: _____ City, state _____ Zip_____
                                    Area code _____ Tel. no._____

Your address at school:_____ Tel. no._____
        City, State, Zip:_____ Area code _____

Height:_____ Wt.:____Age: ____ Marital status:_____Date of birth:_____

Age and sex of children:_____

What type position do you want at camp?  (Junior counselors MUST BE high
school graduates or college freshman, and counselors MUST HAVE completed
sophomore year in college.)_____

From whom did you learn about KANAKUK KAMP and KANAKOMO KAMP?_____
_____

With what age group do you prefer to work at camp?
               LEAVE THIS SPACE BLANK & TURN THE PAGE!
```

1.	2.	3.
		Cat. _____ Acl. _____ _____ _____ Sal. Ofr. _____ Contract Sent _____ Rec'd. _____
_____ R.OP. _____		

Continued.

```
University now                        Class       Activities, athletics
   attending         Major       (Circle one)   honors, positions held, etc.

                                     Freshman
                                     Sophomore
                                     Junior
                                     Senior
                                     Graduate

Summer experience as employee
            Position                              Address           Dates

Last summer:_____   _____  _____

Summer before last: _____   _____  _____

Before that:_____   _____  _____

Camp experience as camper. List honors won, achievements, etc.:_____
_____
_____

References: (list three, including former employers.  Do not list relatives.)
        Names                      Addresses              Positions
_____
_____
_____
_____
_____

What is your religious preference?_____

What Christian work have you been involved in? (Church, F.C.A., Young Life,
Campus Crusade, etc.) _____
_____
_____

What role has Christianity played in your life?  How do you feel about it?
_____

What terms are you available?

        _____ First          _____ Second        _____ Third

Write a brief biographical sketch, including all high school and college
honors and activities, specialized training in camping, experience or
training in other fields which might have a bearing on this application.
Don't be afraid to brag!  Tell us everything, as this part is very
important in your application. (Continued on bottom of next page.)
_____
_____
_____
_____
_____
_____
_____
_____
```

On the following list put number "1" before those activities you can organize and teach __proficiently__; put number "2" before those activities in which you can __assist__ in teaching; and put "3" before those which are just your hobby. (Score these carefully and completely as they have a large bearing on your employment possibilities.)

ARTS AND CRAFTS

_____ Leather work
_____ Indian lore
_____ Painting
_____ Sketching
_____ Wood carving
_____ Woodworking

SPORTS

_____ Archery
_____ Badminton
_____ Baseball
_____ Basketball
_____ Fishing
_____ Football
_____ Tumbling
_____ Horizontal bar
_____ Ping pong
_____ Riflery N.R.A.
_____ Softball
_____ Tennis
_____ Track and field
_____ Volleyball
_____ Trampoline
_____ Wrestling
_____ Weight training
_____ Trap & skeet
_____ Hockey
_____ _____
_____ _____
_____ _____
_____ _____
_____ _____

CAMP CRAFT

_____ Camp craft
_____ Hiking
_____ Outdoor cooking
_____ Overnight camping

DANCING

_____ Ballet
_____ Tap
_____ Modern
_____ Acrobatic

DRAMATICS

_____ Creative
_____ Play directing
_____ Skits & stunts

MISCELLANEOUS

_____ Campfire programs
_____ Evening programs
_____ First aid
_____ Story telling
_____ Worship services

MUSIC

_____ Lead singing
_____ Instruments (list)
_____ _____
_____ _____

NATURE

_____ Animals
_____ Astronomy
_____ Birds
_____ Flowers
_____ Forestry
_____ Trees, rocks, etc.

WATERFRONT ACTIVITIES

_____ Canoeing
_____ Diving
_____ Life saving
_____ Sailing
_____ Swimming
_____ Water ballet
_____ Synchronized
_____ swimming
_____ Water skiing
_____ Boat driving

Do you hold current lifesaving or W.S.I. certificates? _____
Which ones? _____
Other information on activities: _____
_____
_____
_____
_____
_____
_____
_____

Why do you want to work at Kamp? _____
_____
_____

(Biographical sketch continued) _____
_____
_____
_____
_____
_____
_____

(Continue on back if necessary)

Date: _____   Signature: _____

Patience

Each of us wants others to be patient with us. Generally we try to avoid those individuals who have acquired the reputation of being impatient. What is patience? Most of us know only too well what impatience is because it is manifested by some form of overt behavior, but sometimes we find it exceedingly difficult to define exactly what patience *is*.

Webster defines patience as "a state, quality, power, or fact, of being patient." When we look then to the definition of "patient" we discover that it is something that isn't. Again quoting Webster, "patient" means, "bearing or enduring pains, trials, or the like, without complaint, expectant with calmness or without discontent; also, undisturbed by obstacles, delays, failures, etc."

If the counselor is to treat his camper with patience, he should have the ability to hold his temper just one more time; help and explain for the millionth time in the same tone of voice and frame of mind that he used the first time; recognize the camper's limitations and capacities and be willing to take the time to wait for the camper to "measure up"; and have perserverance in a trying situation.

Patience implies taking time. It requires waiting. When the time is up, and waiting proves unproductive, the counselor must step in with firmness and authority. On occasions when such firmness is necessary, the counselor's authoritarianism should always be tempered with recognition of the fact that the camper is a child, not an adult, and that children have the right to take a little longer to "measure up" than adults do.

Kindness

"He is one of the kindest persons I've ever known." What greater tribute could a camper pay a counselor than to describe him as a kind person? One or two acts of kindness would not in themselves merit noteworthy praise, but a person who is basically and genuinely kind is indeed a rare individual and a treasure beyond price to have as a counselor.

Kindness implies unselfishness: the ability to place others ahead of self. Each of us has our own understanding of the significance of the word. When asked to give their opinions, a group of prospective counselors described kindness with the following phrases: just plain being nice to people; something you do because you want to—both you and the receiver should feel better; it's rather like loving one's fellowman, but then extending that love by doing something for him; essentially thinking of the wants of others before your own, doing something good, but not out of any sense of obligation or duty—doing something more than is called for; involves a sensitivity to the needs and feelings of others, and a willingness to meet those needs and respect those feelings—it is a product of love, not duty; unconsciously helping the other person without any thought of reward—maybe by words, actions, or just a simple smile; the unending generation of warmth and real concern for another at all times—it involves facial expressions, tone of voice, and choice of words which convey one's feelings.

As directors and supervisors, we could perhaps do a little better job grammatically in describing kindness, but few of us could capture the truth and depth of this attribute better than the above phrases do. Regardless of our specific choice of words, a definition of kindness must imply unselfishness, giving more than is expected without thought of return, and being motivated by love.

Camping provides unlimited opportunities for teaching children how to live, work, and play with others. We strive to teach campers to be kind to one another. Here is the perfect situation in which the counselor can practice what he preaches. The degree to which th counselor is kind to his campers will determine the degree of kindness his campers will show to others.

So many times we tend to limit our acts of kindness to those who seem to need it most—the homesick child, the unskilled child, the ugly child. But how about the happy child—the "normal, average camper"? Such children are as deserving of the counselor's beyond-the-call-of-duty kindness as other children, and they are very likely to be the ones who receive the least consideration.

In many camps counselors are not permitted to give gifts of monetary value to their campers. This is a good policy. The value of a monetary gift seems much less when one of the greatest and most inexpensive gifts a counselor can bestow upon all of his campers is kindness twenty-four hours a day.

Forgiveness

Human beings are fallible. For this reason, each of us cherishes the hope that others will forgive us when we succumb to our human weakness.

Not infrequently in a discussion involving forgiveness, the question is raised, "Is it possible to *forget* a wrongdoing as well as to forgive the fault?" Counselors need not concern themselves with this psychological dilemma, rather they should be able to forgive the camper and do so with the intent of forgetting the incident. The counselor is more likely to forget the misdeed if he has not used it as a topic of gossip in conversations with other counselors and campers, as in the following instance: The counselor observes Jimmy, alone in the cabin, taking something that does not belong to him from another camper's trunk. Jimmy expresses regret for what he has done and in the discussion with his counselor seems sincerely intent upon not repeating such an incident. This encounter should be the end of the incident. Jimmy is not likely to tell his cabinmates what he did, and the counselor should not repeat to other counselors his knowledge of the wrongdoing. Suspicion of guilt is a deadly thing, and the fewer counselors who know of such an incident, the greater the likelihood that the camper will be able to maintain his self-respect and fight off other temptations that present themselves.

There is something miraculous about the way forgiveness cleanses both the heart and the mind. The ability to forgive and to accept forgiveness is a prerequisite of happiness. The child as well as an adult must be able to forgive himself, and this act of self-forgiveness is made easier if the other person gives every indication that he has completely forgotten about the incident. Too frequently we forgive a child for having done wrong, but by our actions we seem to be waiting to see if there will be a repetition of the misdeed. To return to our example of Jimmy: The counselor should make every effort to have Jimmy feel comfortable in his presence and should be able to convey to Jimmy the feeling that Jimmy need not be ashamed to face him. The camper should feel that the counselor has confidence in him and likes him. If such a warm relationship can exist between the two, then Jimmy is more likely to acquire the social values necessary for successful group living.

A second chance

matter how desperately we strive for perfection, we are going to make mistakes. It
fe to wager that there is not an adult in camping who at one time or another has
le and done so with full knowledge that the rule was being broken. Many
ken rules or made unwise choices with the best intentions to do the cor-
ociety or an individual will deem our behavior inappropriate. Be-
ngs, mistakes will occur, intentionally or otherwise.

When an error occurs, the important consideration is not so much what the fault was, but what the aftereffects will be for the "guilty" individual. We are continuously pleading for A SECOND CHANCE for ourselves—an opportunity to demonstrate that we can do better.

As an example, consider the counselor who comes in late one night following a legitimate time off. His cabin is left unattended at taps. During his unauthorized absence some boys get into a fight, which results in a broken tooth for one of the campers. In view of the fact that an accident occurred in his cabin while he was AWOL should the director fire him the next day? The normal course of action would be for the counselor to ask the director to give him a second chance to prove that he is a responsible individual. Will the director give this counselor a second opportunity and run the risk of having other counselors behave in similar fashion because the word gets around that the director is an "easy mark"? No matter what the director's decision in this case, the counselor will believe that he is entitled to a second chance.

In the typical summer camp, campers are not going to be making the kind of mistakes that would necessitate proceedings for legal action. The camper's mistake will most likely occur because he has no clear-cut set of values to guide his course of action. The question then arises: How will a child acquire values if he is not given a second chance to demonstrate that he is capable of a better course of action?

For many adults the concept of forgiveness is limited to accepting an apology; for many others, forgiveness comes from the vocal chords rather than the heart. It is necessary to point out to these individuals that forgiveness without an accompanying opportunity for a second chance is of little value. Consider for the moment the plight of the man who has served his prescribed time in prison for a wrongdoing. The law says he has paid his debt to society, but does society always give him an opportunity to prove that he has what it takes to become a contributing member and an asset to the "outside" world? We know the answer only too well. The exconvict has a very difficult time being accepted. Too often he is treated as an outcast, an untouchable, a poor risk. Having such a status ascribed to him, is it any wonder that the man becomes a "repeater"?

A camper who has made a mistake should not have to share the same fate as an exconvict. Counselors should recognize that campers are going to make mistakes because it is human and normal. Therefore, campers must be given a second and even a third or fourth chance to demonstrate the ability to acquire social and moral values.

Self-concept

Human beings play many roles in life. We put on these various roles and take them off much like we choose clothes from a wardrobe, selecting what seems appropriate for the occasion. Children sometimes choose inappropriately because they do not know what they have available to choose from or because they lack familiarity with the situation confronting them. They are seeking the answer to questions that often they are not conscious of having asked: Who am I? What am I? Why am I?

In Harry Stack Sullivan's terms when the child behaves "correctly" and is complimented, he sees himself as the *good me;* if he is scolded, he may see himself as *bad me;* if the threat of the situation is too great for him to face the consequences of his behavior, the child may divorce himself from the reality of the situation with the *not me* approach. If there is an accepting attitude toward the self, that attitude will be evident to others. It is not "as ye judge that ye shall be judged," but as you judge yourself so shall you judge others (Sullivan, 1947). Perceptions of self in many situations, together with the objects,

57   *Text continued on p. 62.*

Child growth and development, characteristics and needs*

Ages 8, 9, and 10 years

Physical growth and development

1. Skeletal growth

a. Growth in height and weight are normally slow and steady at this age. There will be a lag just prior to pubescence.

b. Girls have a spurt of growth at about 10 years. They attain skeletal maturity before boys.

c. Differences in individual ossification are very wide, as much as 5 or 6 years at a given age. Malnutrition or serious illness may delay ossification.

d. Mental maturity and social adjustment have some correlation with skeletal maturity.

2. Dentition

a. Permanent dentition continues. Incisors and lower bicuspids appear.

b. This is often a period of dental neglect.

c. Orthodontia (teeth straightening) is necessary in some cases. The need may be apparent as early as 9 years, but treatment may not be initiated until 12 years or later.

3. Muscular development

a. The small muscles are developing. Manipulative skill is increasing.

b. Muscular coordinations are good. The hand-eye coordinations are continuing to develop.

c. Posture may be poor, not even as good as during the first year of school. The spindly type of body is most inclined to droop. In some cases poor posture may be symptomatic. Its presence may indicate a condition needing attention: chronic infection, fatigue, orthopedic difficulties, emotional maladjustment, etc.

Characteristics

1. The child of 8, 9, or 10 years is sturdy though long-legged and rangy in appearance. His health is usually good and he has boundless energy. He seems hurried and untidy. He is prone to accidents.

2. He now has a wider range of interests and a longer attention span. His goals are immediate and consistency is demanded, as individual justice.

3. He is learning to cooperate better. He plays in self-made groups over a longer period. He is beginning to be interested in teams and will abide by group decisions.

4. The child desires prestige and may seek it through size, boasting, and rivalry.

5. The rhythmic sense is much improved.

6. Sex antagonism may be acute. Sex interest is not detailed. Sexual "modesty" appears.

7. The appetite is good. The child is interested in eating. There are fewer food preferences and refusals.

8. He is generally reliable about following instructions in household jobs. He can take care of his own room.

9. He can take responsibility for his own clothing. He is now more aware of his personal hygiene.

Needs

1. The child needs an assured position in a social group. Membership in a gang or a secret club fills this need. At this period children need a certain amount of freedom in setting up their own standards and rules, yet strongly desire understanding and sympathy from adults. Participation in family affairs is important.

2. There must be full opportunity to develop body control, strength, and endurance. The child of 8, 9, or 10 years needs activities involving use of the whole body: stunts, throwing and catching, running "it" games with their accompanying noise, etc. Seasonal play is important: kites, tops, marbles, etc.

3. He needs organized games for team play. He is willing to practice in order to become adequate in skills for games. He gains self-confidence by excelling in some one thing.

4. It is as important for children to learn good followership as it is for them to learn good leadership.

5. Encouragement to exercise creativity in rhythms should be given.

6. Activities such as playing in caves and brooks, gathering nuts, making campfires are needed. Bicycles and skates are enjoyed.

7. The child should sleep about 10 hours. He usually does not get enough rest. A quiet period in the afternoon, not necessarily bed, may prevent over-fatigue.

8. The child's increased interest in foods provides a basis for better understanding of the seven basic foods in maintaining good health.

9. The teacher must see that pupils having visual or aural defects always maintain strategic positions in the class.

10. Close supervision is required to assure properly adjusted furniture and to prevent slumping over desks. Creation of an awareness that good posture is comfortable posture is important.

58

4. Organic development
   a. The heart develops in size less rapidly than the body. Its work is increased. Damage to the heart is prevented during play because the skeletal muscles fatigue first. Taxing the heart should be avoided by seeing that children do not compete with those who are stronger or more mature physically.
   b. The lungs are not fully developed.
   c. At the end of this period the eyes function as well as those of adults. Myopia (near-sightedness) may develop around the age of 8 years. Many eye defects can be remedied by glasses.
   d. By the end of this period the child will have had many of the contagious diseases of childhood or will have built up immunity to them. The linear-type child is more susceptible to tuberculosis, a prevalent disease of childhood.
   e. Internal changes in glands and body structure are taking place. There is a wide range in the beginning of sexual maturity. The period of rapid growth comes earlier for girls than for boys. It lasts longer in boys.
      Boys: Beginning of puberty cycle: 10-13 yrs.
      End: 14-18-½ yrs.
      Girls: Appearance of menstruation: 10-16 yrs.
      Average: 13 yrs.

Physical growth and development
1. Skeletal growth
   a. This is a transitional period.
   b. During the "pubescent spurt" the rate of growth is very rapid. The lateral-type matures earlier than the linear-type.

Ages 11, 12, and 13 years

Characteristics
1. Children of 11, 12, or 13 years are strongly individual. They differ widely in physical maturity and in temperament.
2. The lateral-type child may display overweight, slow and placidity. The linear-type child may display drooping posture, fatigue, alternating alertness and irritability.

Needs
1. There must be careful supervision in order that children of these ages may choose games proportionate to their strength and appropriate for their developmental needs.
2. Skill is essential for successful group participation. The child is willing to practice skills to gain proficiency, but needs informed guidance.

Continued.

---

*Charts developed by Public Schools of the District of Columbia Curriculum Committee for Health, Physical Education, and Safety.

Child growth and development, characteristics and needs—cont'd

Ages 11, 12, and 13 years—cont'd

Physical growth and development

  c. At 11 years, girls are usually taller and heavier than boys. Boys' hands and feet appear to be oversized.

2. Dentition

  a. Permanent dentition of 28 teeth is completed by 13 or 14 years.

  b. For those who need it, orthodontia will improve the appearance and prevent dental decay. The child needs guidance about accepting embarrassment and discomfort to achieve permanent correction.

3. Muscular development

  a. Muscular growth is very rapid. Restlessness may be a concomitant.

  b. Poor control will ensue if the body framework and muscular development are out of proportion in their rate of growth.

  c. Posture may be slovenly. Awkwardness is prevalent.

4. Organic development

  a. The heart is not growing as rapidly as the body.

  b. The blood pressure may fall. The fatigue point in competitive games should be anticipated. More rest is needed.

  c. There are many minor illnesses of short duration.

  d. The puberty cycle is in progress. The reproductive organs are maturing rapidly. Secondary sex characteristics appear. Many girls are embarrassed by the development of breasts and hips. The period of changing voice and initial hair growth on the face is equally embarrassing to boys.

Characteristics

3. The increase in size and strength of muscles leads to greater interest in outdoor activities.

4. Competition is keen. There is respect for good sportsmanship. More highly organized team games are desired. There is a willingness to submerge personal ego for the good of the team or group. The unskilled child is self-conscious about undertaking new activities.

5. Some children may initiate too many activities and go beyond the fatigue point. Resultant chronic tension may cause strained relationships. Girls tire more readily than boys.

6. There is a shift to own-age codes. Prestige is more important than adult approval. The gang interest is changing to interest in one or two "best" friends.

7. Interest in money-making activities may lead some to work during after-school playtime.

8. There is a strong interest in sex. These children may be emotional about bodily changes. Sex-consciousness may cause self-consciousness and shyness with the opposite sex. Teasing may denote sex attraction.

9. A ravenous but capricious appetite may be noted.

10. The child may be overanxious about his own health. He appreciates first aid and can give it. To a certain extent he can appreciate group health problems.

Needs

3. Games of increased organization such as softball, kickball, modified soccer, etc., are needed. The sedentary or self-protective child may need encouragement to play out-of-doors. Differentiation of activities for boys and girls may begin at these ages.

4. Special provision must be made for the child who is reaching his literate capacity and may be able to gain his chief satisfactions from muscular activities.

5. It is as important for children to develop good spectatorship as it is for them to develop good sportsmanship.

6. More mature interests must be met by more mature programs. There must be opportunity for many types of social contacts. Club programs, church groups, Boy and Girl Scouts, YMCA, Campfire Girls, and camping, etc., fill the need for guidance.

7. Provision must be made for a growing interest in social dancing.

8. The rest needs are about 8 to 9 hours or longer.

9. The child's increasing desire to improve his personal appearance provides excellent opportunity to remedy habitual postural defects and to establish a balanced diet.

60

Physical growth and development

1. Skeletal growth
   a. The girls are about 2 years ahead of boys at this age.
   b. The lateral-type girl usually reaches adult height at about the age of 14 years. Linear-type girls continue to grow for several years. The lateral-type boy attains adult height at about the age of 16 years. Growth of linear-type boys continues to the age of 20 or later.
   c. Bone growth is completed with sexual maturity.
   d. The face and body are now attaining adult contours.
2. Dentition
   a. A few children cut third molars (wisdom teeth) at the end of this period, but this is usually deferred for a number of years.
   b. Dental correction continues to be one of the greatest needs of childhood.
3. Muscular development
   a. The awkward age is ending. There is improvement in coordination.
   b. The muscles of boys become hard and firm. The muscles of girls remain softer.
   c. Posture is improving. Control and grace are displayed, especially by those who have participated in rhythmic activities such as dancing, swimming, and sports.
4. Organic development
   a. The heart increases greatly in size. Boys and girls should avoid strenuous competitive sports since the heart and arteries may be out of proportion.
   b. The puberty cycle is completed in the majority of cases.
   c. There may be a period of glandular instability with fluctuations in energy level. Ailments of this age may include headache, nosebleed, "nervousness," palpitations, and acne.
   d. The prevalence of active tuberculosis increases in the teen-ager.

Characteristics

1. The child of 14, 15, or 16 may have reached physiological adulthood, but lacks its experiences. He may exhibit a "know-it-all" attitude. He is intensely emotional. He is seeking his own place in the life around him. There may be emotional instability while striving to understand social relationships.
2. The desire to conform to standards of the age group is stronger than the response to adult guidance. Many respond more readily to the influence of the teacher than of the parent.
3. During adolescence there may be close attachment to and almost unlimited admiration of some adult whom he considers to be outstanding.
4. All can compete in games requiring higher skills. Groups evolve according to physical maturation and interests.
5. Boys like to be thought big, strong, and healthy. Girls desire prettiness. In both sexes there is interest in physical attractiveness and good grooming. However, because of a strong desire for uniformity, studied oddities in dress may be followed by all for some time.
6. Wage-earning is desired by many.
7. Sexual manifestations may cause self-consciousness. Because of differences in maturity of the sexes at this level, girls are more interested in boys than boys are in girls. Many lack adequate sex information and guidance. Sexual delinquency may be caused by a feeling of nonbelonging in the home and the desire for other ties.
8. The appetite is enormous at this age, yet there is a tendency toward an inadequate breakfast or none at all. Overdeveloped girls may become intrigued by "reducing" diets.
9. The child may become overconfident about assuming personal responsibility for maintaining good health. He has an understanding of the nature of disease. He readily uses first aid. He is interested in community health problems.

Needs

1. Children of 14, 15, or 16 need unobtrusive adult guidance that does not impinge upon their own feelings of being adults. A balance between security and freedom is needed.
2. Family solidarity as a retreat from the confusion of widened horizons and more complex experiences is important.
3. Children of this age need worthy causes in the promulgation of which they may utilize their excess emotions and energy.
4. Separate physical education programs for boys and girls should be planned since the difference in strength, maturity, and interests makes it difficult to organize activities beneficial to both. Boys follow youth sports. In addition to group games, girls like smaller group activities, to be carried on by two or more people.
5. Special provision must be made for the child who is reaching his literate capacity and may be able to gain his chief satisfactions from muscular activities.
6. Social dancing is a "must" at this level.
7. Rest needs are about the same as for adults, 8 hours or longer.
8. School and community must unite to plan with and for these young people a worthwhile after-school program. The place and the activities must be agreeable to them. Provision must be made for the child who desires creative, manipulative, or contemplative activities, as well as for those who wish more active recreation.

people, ideas, and values that he views as part or characteristic of himself, constitute the child's self-concept. The individual's sense of self may be healthy (normal?), withdrawn, aggressive, and so on. Another way of putting it is that the individual adjusts to the environment by compromise (substitution), withdrawal (flight, fear), or attack (aggression, hostility). Compromise is the most common method of adjustment to the environment. This may mean accepting substitute goals or lowering one's level of aspiration.

Fundamental desires

In addition to basic biological needs, human beings have fundamental desires that motivate their behavior. These desires are found in all persons but the importance placed upon them varies with the individual. A brief description of these desires is given below. Add your own descriptive words to the list.

1. *The desire for recognition*, which includes social approval, prestige, status, and commendation. It causes the child to seek situations in which these rewards are found and to avoid situations that result in ridicule, scorn, or disapproval.
2. *The desire for affection*, which includes appreciation, understanding, intimacy, and support. The child will avoid situations in which there is lack of love and appreciation.
3. *The desire for power*, which includes a sense of achievement, success, and mastery, results in the avoidance of situations involving frustration and a sense of failure. Some individuals set their levels low to avoid failure. Must experience success.
4. *The desire for new experience*, which includes novelty, adventure, excitement, thrill, and change, causes avoidance of situations of dullness, monotony, and boredom.
5. *The desire for security*, which includes protection, confidence, and optimism, brings about avoidance of situations of fear, apprehension, danger, insecurity, and pessimism. Security is not a place but a person.

Characteristics of different age groups

The focal point of the camp program is the whole child. To understand and relate effectively with his campers, the counselor must know the physical, mental, emotional, and social characteristics and needs of the various age groups. Such knowledge is essential for program planning also. The child growth and development charts on pp. 58 to 61 provide a framework for a better understanding of why children do what they do.

To do

On the basis of the Child Growth and Development Chart and your outside reading, give examples of general camp activities and specific cabin activities appropriate for each age category. See opposite page.

Perception: a look at the camper

The guidelines and questions listed below provide the counselor with provocative material to better understand campers and others.*

1. No two people see things the same way:
   How must I communicate in order that we will:
   a. give a minimum of his own unrelated interpretations to what "I say"?
   b. have the opportunity to "tell" me what he "heard" me say?

---

*Laurence J. Taylor, NFBA *Workbook for Seminar Participants.*

Ages	General camp activities	Specific cabin activities
8, 9, 10 years		
11, 12, 13 years		
14, 15, 16 years		

2. He thinks, feels and sees things anecdotally:
   How do I best learn about his past experiences, background of knowledge, greatest achievements and his interests?
3. He doesn't see things the same way at different times:
   How can I best determine his state of mind, mood, attitude, etc., in order to find the best time to speak with him?
4. He learned to see things as he does:
   How can I best *teach* in order to improve or facilitate his perception of the situation as I see it or as it should be seen?
5. He sees things often not as they are, but as he is:
   How can I best learn about him—his values, interests, problems—in order to better understand his way of seeing things?
6. He sees things largely as he saw them before:
   How do I learn about those things familiar to him which may have an important relationship to the problem at hand?
7. He sees what he is looking for:
   How can I best learn about his anticipations—wishes, hopes, expectations, pre-judgments?
8. He tends to complete those things which appear incomplete:
   How can I communicate so clearly and completely that he will get the "whole picture", not necessitating that he complete it with his own notions, ideas, "facts"?
9. He tends to simplify those things which he does not understand:
   How can I sell a task as important and then check on his mastery of the information or skill as relates to the task?
10. His image of himself largely determines what he will see:
    How can I learn how he sees himself; evaluates himself in terms of worth, compares himself with others?

11. The meanings he receives from me are largely determined by his "image" of me:
How can I best check up on the accuracy of his image of me?
12. First he sees a stimulus as a general pattern, then he focuses his attention on a particular aspect of it:
How can I find out what he considers the "apple of his eye"—the main thing he sees—on which he focuses his attention, to begin his perception?
13. He tends to give sharper attention to the first and the last in a series of things:
How can I take advantage of serial order in both organizing and presenting my communication?
14. Our emotional reactions to others and to ourselves often are barriers to effective perception:
How can I detect his feelings and attitudes when I communicate with him?
15. He shapes new perceptions only through new experience:
(Experiences will be new to him when he permits them to be new.)
How can I communicate most effectively in order to get him to find the self-discipline to enter into new experiences with a sense of enthusiasm and anticipation—even when the new is difficult and even irksome?

Questions to ask yourself after you have attempted to help a camper solve a problem:
1. Did I really understand how he perceives the problem?

2. Did I understand how emotionally involved he is with the problem?

3. Did I deal with the problem as a shared exploration?

4. Was I able to help him identify the resources he has to solve the problem?

5. What questions did I ask that were particularly helpful to him?

6. How well did I say what I meant?

The three L's of childhood

All human beings, especially children, must be provided the three L's. In contrast to the bygone three R's of school days, we may refer to these as the three L's of Childhood.

love   feeling of affection, worth, appreciation.
This L provides the umbrella under which the entire maturation process must take place. Love the child gently and loosely—do not smother or squeeze.

limits   must be appropriate to the maturation level of the child. Must be constant and not fluctuate as if they were on hinges and dependent upon the humor of the adult.

liberty   within clearly defined limits the child must be given liberty to choose, be successful, make mistakes, learn responsibility, and accept the consequences of his behavior.

An additional *L* that is sometimes suggested is *Listen*. Listen to children. They can teach us much.

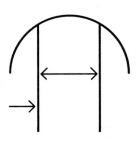

Individual versus group

So many of the activities and reasons for doing things at camp are for the welfare of the group. This is as it should be since a camp is a social setting. However, a word of caution is needed. *Don't lose sight of individual campers.* A child's needs and interests must be met. The counselor should not lose sight of the camper's right to *individuality.* Well-adjusted individuals make for better group structure.

A good counselor

To help solve camper and staff problems, the counselor must have the courage to admit he may be wrong; avoid deliberately embarrassing a child; remembers that all people have emotions; realize that our physical and mental conditions are linked (when tired, hungry, or hurried is not a time to solve children's problems); watch the spur-of-the-moment reactions (think first, act second); and know that a child is won by being asked, not told; know some simple formula for problem solving:

Just what is the problem?
Why does it exist?
How can it be solved—all possible solutions? Let's try the best solutions.
Did it work? Why or why not?

> *For all the countless famous things,*
> *The wondrous record-breaking things,*
> *These never-can-be-equalled things*
> *That all the papers cite.*
>
> *Are not the little human things,*
> *The "everyday encountered" things,*
> *The "just-because-I-like-you" things,*
> *That make us happy quite.*
>
> *So here's to all the little things,*
> *The "done-and-then-forgotten" things,*
> *Those "ah-it's-simply-nothing things"*
> *That make life worth the fight.*
>
> *"The Friendly Things"*
> *Van B. Harper*

Techniques
Thumbnail sketch

Many a camp director has directed counselors to write a thumbnail sketch of each camper under their supervision. "Just a short thumbnail sketch." What goes into it is left to the counselor's imagination because the scanty direction indicates that everyone knows what the term "thumbnail sketch" means.

This simple technique serves in more than one way. The counselor writes a very short description of the camper that provides a definite impression. The counselor is directed to consider more than the camper's physical characteristics. The counselor attempts to get an impression of the camper's personality, of his ability to be himself, and of his first relationships with other campers and adults at camp. This technique requires the counselor take a close look at each child.

Thumbnail sketches should be written at the first of each week so that they are not entirely based on first impressions. They should then become part of the camper's permanent record file. Weekly sketches should show signs of change due to the counselor's familiarity with the camper, the child's actual personal maturation, and the counselor's improved ability to see maturation and change. Such information in a personal permanent record file would be valuable to the camper's counselor the following summer.

Use of the thumbnail sketch technique provides a camp director with a marvelous opportunity to assist the counselor in his ability to understand and work with children. The grammar and punctuation may leave something to be desired, but the counselor's perception, or lack of it, is revealed to himself and to the director. By working together they will be better able to provide maximum opportunity for a camper's personal growth.

The following samples of a thumbnail sketch show the perceptions of young, inexperienced counselors. The sketches *have not been edited* except to change the camper's name.

> Karen, our cabin vice president, is a little girl who gives a first and lasting impression of being lovable. Her spirit of cooperation and friendliness has often been exhibited in the cabin. Karen well deserved the sabre she received at the last pirate council and the jewel for continued work which she is going to receive this week.
>
> Jeannette is a lively young miss full of ideas good and mischievous. Her enthusiasm sometimes leads her in the wrong direction. The past few days Jeannette has been carrying her new white rabbit everywhere she goes. This and other actions lead me to believe that Jeannette needs kind direction and will respond to as much kindness as is given her.
>
> Sarah is a smart little lady who forms very definite opinions. She may change them from day to day but when she has one she doesn't hesitate to express it. She is a model for the rest of the cabin in her neatness of appearance, manner, and living. She has shown definite growth in group living even in the few weeks that I have known her. Her usually helpful manner and attitude have made her deserving of the sabre she will receive this week.
>
> Martha is a slender gal with very expressionate eyes. The sad idea of it is that very often the beautiful eyes meant for happiness express sullenness, boredom, or rebellion. At first Martha was slow at her cabin duties but lately she seems to be improving. If she finds something that she enjoys doing she has enough stick-to-itiveness to finish. I believe that Martha's background, one of the main factors being the death of her father, has affected her life greatly. In the future, she will need continued prodding but to have it be effective it must be done by someone she admires and loves.
>
> Quiet, gentle, and unassuming is our Gerry. Seldom do you hear her laugh or even talk. If and when she does it hardly ever is around older people. She seems to enjoy herself though and takes part in all activities. She never lacks in cabin cooperation, and the other day out in the rowboat showed real determination in moving those oars. I would like to work further with this little girl and bring her out of herself.
>
> Sandy is a chubby little girl full of fun. She has not yet learned to take care of her clothes and hair and is therefore usually messy. The other campers seem to realize this and because of it she is not always so popular. Her slowness requires constant attention for if she is not kept after she would be left behind in most events. Despite this her cheerful nature makes her a little sweetheart.
>
> A tiny one is Paula. If she receives constant attention she is smiling and happy but if the attention drifts away from herself for a long time she begins to pout and tears may fall. Paula is well known to most people in camp because of her darling smile and elfish way. With proper guidance Paula will overcome her spoiledness and become a better camper.
>
> Jackie is a stocky miss with a round face and devilish eyes. She is the cabin president but not a real leader. If properly motivated Jackie can be the fastest worker in the cabin and a big help but if the doldrums set in, watch out. She says "no" quite readily and can be very stubborn. When in this mood she takes correction in a sulking way. Jackie is a camper with whom I would like to spend a great deal of time as I believe she presents a challenge and has possibilities.

66

Jane is a very friendly and cooperative child, but extremely slow in her actions and manner of accomplishing anything. She is well adjusted to the camp situation.

Magda is a patient and thoughtful girl worthy of confidence. She has a quiet way of accepting persons or situations which has a definite calming effect on the cabin as a whole. She is well liked by the other girls.

I think of Sally as being a little old lady. She is selfish in her actions and tends to boss the other girls. She needs training in understanding the rights of others.

Laura is a "ball of fire." She presents quite a challenge for any individual. Her mannerisms are her own and she might bite you one minute and love and crawl all over you the next. She is an overly friendly child, quite often late to class because she has felt a need to stop and chat along the way. I like Laura, for I feel that she is someday going to be a leader, but first she will have to settle down and find a set of good habits to follow.

Everybody loves Gloria! Perhaps it is because she is so little and so full of the junior pep. She is improving constantly in attaining a sense of responsibility, begging to fulfill her jobs to her capacity. She is fun to be around, I enjoy her overly worked imagination, although at times she mistakes her dreams for the truth. The camp as a unit likes and seeks her companionship.

Bonnie is a leader who works from underneath, when a situation for buddies comes up everyone in the cabin wants her for a buddy. They seem to consider this quite a privilege. She is very adaptable and well adjusted to group or camp life, and loyal to a situation.

Lisa is an independent sort of girl. She acts a bit older than some of the others and is rather motherly toward some of the shy ones.

Anne is very bossy. She is very fussy about her clothes and belongings. She is homesick usually every time her parents come to see her, which is at least once a week.

Carolyn is very grown up for her age in some ways and young in others. She is not as co-ordinated as some of the others and at times seems to feel it. She is popular with the rest of the campers.

Judy is very much a child. She tries to get away with as much as she can. She doesn't do anything she can get out of. She isn't as friendly toward the rest of the cabin as she could be.

Joyce is apt to be a bit sneaky at times. She doesn't like responsibilities. She is hard to get to know. She is going through a stage in which she thinks, talks, etc. about boys.

Jessica, because of her bad eye, sometimes feels different from the others. She is very sweet and sincere toward all the group, and is very responsible."

Diary reports

It is the rare female who gets through life without having kept a diary. During special periods of time, such as war, it is not unusual for a man to record events and impressions in a special little book. Such a log of events, usually kept on a daily basis, records events, feelings, and even secrets.

A camp counselor can use the diary technique in observing a camper and in getting to know him or her. The counselor needs some sort of notebook, spiral or otherwise, in which he can record his daily observations. He should have a special book kept for this purpose alone. Likewise, he should have a special place to keep the notebook; to keep the campers from discovering its contents.

Unlike the diary kept for personal reasons, the camp counselor's diary on a camper should contain *no* personal interpretation of an incident, nor should there be any attempt to diagnose the *why* of the camper's overt behavior. Rather, it should be a record of a *fact that describes* an action or the behavior of the camper—nothing more.

Correct entry	*Poor entry*
Sue helped Mary make her bed.	Sue was very helpful and assisted Mary today.
Sue cried when her team lost the swimming meet.	Sue seemed terribly upset when her team lost. (I think she feels she caused them to lose)

Record the fact without indicating personal feelings. These facts can then be scrutinized at the end of a designated time interval to determine if a pattern of behavior is revealed through the statements in the diary. The next logical step would be to write a case study based upon data contained in the diary.

Case study

Fortified with pertinent information from the application blank and any other records made available and with the diary report, the counselor is now ready to sit down and write a case study.

Young or inexperienced counselors are quick to draw conclusions. If they are asked to justify their comments on the basis of evidence accumulated in the diary report, they become much more aware that off-the-cuff decisions are not only unfair but are frequently untrue. One cough does not have to be diagnosed as pneumonia nor does lack of a smile mean homesickness is setting in.

In the Counselor Education Program at the National Music Camp, the counselors-in-training are asked to select one camper in their cabin to observe, to keep a diary of their observations, and to prepare a case study on the child based upon the diary. Through the years it has been consistently true that at the completion of the case study most CIT's find that the child they selected was a normal, healthy camper doing exactly what is typical of his age group. Many a counselor-in-the-making has been relieved to discover this truth through his own efforts.

Not infrequently, a young or inexperienced counselor will possess such a keen desire to be a good counselor that he becomes unnecessarily wary, cautious, and suspicious. He draws conclusions based on little evidence because he believes it is necessary for him to come up with a diagnosis of a problem that a camper is presenting. In actual practice the camper must be given a fair chance by the counselor, and vice versa.

The case study will prevent a counselor from making judgments which cannot be supported by repetitive incidents. "Sally is kind." This statement would be backed by the fact that she loaned Sue her swimming cap on Monday. The same day she offered to help Joan find her barrette. At supper time she waited to walk with Ann, who is always the last one out of the cabin. These three incidents support the statement, "Sally is kind."

A study of an extremely nervous child may have much supporting data on record from the family, the school, the church, or the medical doctor. If the child is a "repeater," past camp records will serve as a starting point. The opinion might read "Jack is restless." The diary would perhaps include, "He did not finish his cabin chore but moved about in the cabin talking and getting in the way of the other campers. He played with his breakfast food, leaving it unfinished. He hopped on one foot and then the other as we all walked back to the cabin. He asked John to play ball with him and because John was slow, Jack ran off to get George to play with him and then changed his mind about playing ball. In swimming he would listen to part of the instruction, start to do it, and then change to something else. This happened repeatedly." Thus, evidence that "Jack is restless" accumulates and shows the statement to be factual.

At the conclusion of the case study the counselor may be able to indicate in short, concise terms a fairly accurate profile of a camper. An example of such a summary follows: "In my opinion X's qualities can be described as follows:

Positive	*Negative*	*Other characteristics*
Conscientious	Antagonistic	Moody
Unselfish	Restless (at times)	Good sense of humor
Extremely cooperative	Sulky	Sympathetic
Adjusts to situations easily		Apologetic
Friendly		

In writing the case study a sense of humor on the part of a counselor will provide a leveling off agent when it comes to evaluation. Revealing a sense of humor immediately shows the director that the counselor is a warm, observant, outgoing man or woman—the kind we need so desperately in camping.

Samples of humorous lead-ins to serious discussions follow:

Completely floored—this was my first reaction to Alice, as she fell through the door that first day. While I was alone unpacking, I heard someone singing to herself and glanced out the window. A young girl with rather hunched shoulders, owly glasses and frizzy hair, doing some sort of jitterbug, came up the walk snapping her fingers. I whipped around when I heard the clatter to see Alice sprawled on the floor—she had missed the top step. I knew then that this was my case study.

Although she can give the impression that she is a "normal" thirteen-year-old girl when she wants to, I would not say that Alice is average. Even her home life is not like that of my other campers.

Brown eyes sparkled at me from a freckled face topped by carrot red hair. A warm friendly smile spread from ear to ear revealed several vacant spaces where teeth had yet to come in—"my picket fence smile"—the owner of this face described it. I was immediately struck by her brightness revealed continually in her witty conversation and excellent vocabulary.

'May I call you Norma?' A bright eyed junior camper looked up at me with mischief sparkling in her large brown eyes and with two dimples accenting an infectious smile as she uttered these words. This was my introduction to Suzy. Dressed in blue jeans and a tee shirt and standing at least a full head taller than her cabin mates, she appeared a boyish and natural youngster. Already she was the cabin leader. . . . The birds slept later than Suzy did the next morning and by reveille she was bubbling over with her enthusiasm for the new day. . . . Mealtime passed noisily with Suzy slurping and gulping her food, pushing and shoving her cabin mates. Bedtime arrived and she again interrupted every other word in a loud voice. Finally raising her hand she announced she would like to make a speech. Wiggling self-consciously and observing her toes with great interest as she drew circles on the floor, she muttered, I think we have the two best counselors in camp and I think we should do everything we can to help them. Last year we gave Norma a hard time, but let's not do the same to Dee and Irene this year. She tumbled back into bed in embarrassment and I tucked her in, she whispered in my ear, 'Did you like my little speech?'

The following examples are studies done by young people eighteen and nineteen years of age. The reader will no doubt be aware of a certain freshness and goodness in these statements. Perhaps it is because they are written by young people still very close to the age they are writing about. Because of this closeness a special kind of understanding is evident. Rarely is hopelessness or resignation expressed.

The reader is reminded that no attempt has been made to alter these case studies, other than to remove names. Nor have the authors attempted to analyze the accuracy of the counselor's conclusions regarding a specific camper's adjustment in camp. The studies are offered as examples of what can be accomplished through directed observation.

Case studies based on a four week observation period

CASE 1

Diary report

June 28 Arrived with Mother and sister.
Said little at first.
Asked, "Is there any time for reading at all?"
"I've been told that if you can't say something nice about somebody you shouldn't say anything" (self-righteously.)
Was upset because couldn't find things in her trunk, which we had rearranged.
Twice "refused" (by not taking any) to eat three bites of everything.

June 29 "I was afraid that this would be an awful strict camp."
Ate some of everything.
In filling out a blank, she asked, "Do you have to put your father's name if he's dead?"
Repeatedly wanted to hold my hand, walk with me, etc.
Trunk locked by accident.
Acquiescent when asked to go to bed instead of curling her hair.

June 30 Ready early to go to class, but was confused and whined because she didn't understand where to go.
Took no part in cabin elections.
Continued to want to hold my hand and sit next to me.
Repacked trunk to suit herself.
Enthusiastic about classes.
Finished her part of clean-up early and sat on bed while others worked. (Needed help in finding places to dust.)
First to volunteer to help counselor.
Ready early to have hair curled.

July 1 Readily gave up seat by me at lunch when someone else asked her to do so.
Said "I need a Daddy" when talk turned to our Junior Girls' Dad.
First to clap for those elected as newspaper representatives.

July 2 Braided part of her own hair.
Repacked trunk meticulously.
"It's all right to make fun of people if you do it in a nice way."
Read while others played.
Whined when she had to go to bed early, but was the first ready.
Several times teased and made jokes for the first time.

July 3 Very upset when someone cut in ahead of her in line.
Braided own hair without being asked to do so.
Hung up bathing suits for others.

July 4 Very cross in the morning—made snappish remarks with little provocation.
Much concerned over my being slightly ill.
When others wished that two sick girls were back, she countered, "But they'll get better care in the infirmary."
Very, very tired, almost nervous exhaustion.

July 5   My day off as well as breakfast cookout.

July 6   "That's enough smarty pants!" when slightly irritated.
Was one of four to stay in the cabin to do extra volunteer clean-up.
Wanted written I.O.U. for money loaned to a friend.
Helped others set their hair.
Evening: Upset by something, probably by being accused of cheating in Mother May I?
She withdrew almost completely: ran back to the cabin, walked behind the group, cried
silently. Sat by herself at the playground and refused to admit or discuss what was
wrong when encouraged to do so. Finally "thawed out" and was happy in store and on
merry-go-round. When next observed she was repelling the advances of the other cam-
pers: "Keep your opinions to yourself."
"I hate Grace." (This when forced to wait for her.)
Jerked away when Karla tried to put her arm around her.
Refused my offer of Kleenex casually slipped into her hand, which she had accepted
before. Admitted to Pat that she was very lonely.

July 7   Fairly cheerful.
Insisted on repacking trunk and thus failed to help in cabin clean-up.
Will be a princess with Polly.
Said that her day had been pretty good.

July 8   Very happy, even "bubbly."
Sharp comments had an underlying happiness to take out sting.
Failed to get sweeping done in time for class.
Spent time with Polly and friend from cabin nine.
Still refused to go in swimming because it's too cold.
Included in cabin secret society.
Didn't want to participate in a special interest group.
Still inclined to stick to herself.

July 9   Sitting on Polly's bed when I got up, and walked out arm-in-arm with her. Excited about
craft work and also two new books sent by her Mother. Still clings to me in walking,
etc.

July 10   Didn't get bed made before breakfast and read instead of sweeping right away.
Had to be begged to go in swimming—still gets too cold.
Buddied with a girl from another cabin.

July 11   Vomited in night without getting out of bed "because I forgot to go to the bathroom."
Seemed all right otherwise.
Wished that she didn't have to work hard to get an award.

July 12   Came to breakfast late with Mary and Polly. Insisted that she must clean her trunk before
she did cabin duties.
Fixed her own hair. Mother came to visit, but missed her reaction since it was my day off.

July 13   Insisted on having hair set twice.
Didn't want to play outdoors in the afternoon or ride in a boat with the others at the car-
nival.

July 14   Now first to sleep and last to wake up, in reverse of original actions.
Another reversal: Signed up for boating, and wanted to go in swimming. (Weather was
much warmer.)
Very disappointed when told that in the future she would have to do her own hair up, but
did a good job of it.

July 15   Greeted me with a big hug while I was still in bed. Got sweeping done early. I left for overnight.

July 16   Held my hand on the way to meals still, "Do we have to sleep on the tennis courts Friday night?"

Complained when others made noise so that she couldn't read during rest hour.

Upset because she had to wait for the whole cabin to leave for dinner, and offered to hang up all bathing suits to hurry us along.

July 17   *I'm* not going to wear a sweater to class.

Wanted to clear line to complete duties, even though it inconvenienced others to bring in wet suits.

Read when finished cabin duties.

"Oh, I like the water now."

"Chummed" with a number of different girls.

Case study

I immediately became interested in my small, blond, ten-year-old case study when she asked her first question after a shy and silent arrival, "Is there *any* time for reading at all?" Succeeding days have uncovered many interesting facets of her personality in addition to her enjoyment of reading.

What little I know of her family background might account for some of her reactions. She has lost her father, rather recently I believe, which may be a partial cause of her loneliness. She has one sister about seven years older than she, which makes her the "baby" of the family. This seems to lead naturally to her greater than average immaturity, her expectation of more than ordinary attention from adults, and her tendency to want to have things without working for them. These traits appear in her lack of a sense of group and sometimes self-responsibility, as well as her attitude toward awards.

Her family training seems to be on high standards, and while it now conflicts with selfishness of action at times, it will probably triumph in the end in her actions as well as in her words. (Note her remarks about being nice to others, her disturbance upon being caught cheating, and occasional extra help in the cabin—in most cases for rather selfish motives—in contrast to the desire to fix her hair, trunk, etc. before fulfilling cabin duties.) This conflict is only natural, however, for one of her age.

As mentioned above, the fact that she is the youngest in her family means that she is probably around older people more than her peers. This is evident in her great dependence on counselors. The desire for adult comradeship, however, is natural for her age group. My camper does have special areas of unusual maturity, however. With proper channeling, her desire to be self-sufficient and her growing ability along this line, as well as her systematic care of her possessions, will prove valuable to her, especially when she overcomes her lack of practice in doing things for herself. Another help would be for her to lose her great sensitivity to supposed criticism.

My case study has had to make a great adjustment both to camping and sports activities and to learning to find her place in the cabin group. Until she found one or two special friends she was very unhappy. Her classes seem to have been a helpful, stabilizing factor in that they were enjoyed for themselves and have given opportunity for the beginning of new friendships. Since she has made one or two friends, she has somewhat left behind her introversion and branched out into new friendships with increased self-confidence. Her adjustment to camping activities has been a slow one, but practice and the weather have encouraged new interests to the point that she is enthusiastic about many activities.

She seems to fit the general characteristics of her age group rather well. With only a few exceptions, she has gone with the group in "gang" activities. She is very interested in reading, likes adult comradeship, and has developed some interest in abstract concepts and feelings. She expresses all five of the fundamental desires to a high degree with the exception of the desire for new experience.

To summarize, I should say that my case study shows very good development as a camper and promises good future growth. She seems to have ended her period of withdrawal from the group and is now learning both self-sufficiency and group-cooperation. Her natural generosity, ability to learn quickly, and great determination to do what she sets out to do are great assets. Qualities such as impatience and forgetfulness are natural and will be outgrown. To me, she is a natural, fairly happy and very lovable camper.

CASE 2

Case study (Diary report omitted)

Elaine is eleven and a half years old. She lives with her parents and two sisters, aged fourteen and eighteen. The younger is presently in camp here. She attends private school. Her father is a merchant; her mother, a teacher. She says of Elaine, "I am hoping she will learn the value of the give and take situation that is so much a part of camp life. Elaine is quite a volatile and energetic child, and she needs to learn how to properly channel her energy." With this in mind we will look at Elaine.

Elaine is the problem girl in the cabin. She is rude to her cabin mates and to her counselors, she creates chaos and promotes disunity in the cabin, she is defiant and defensive and will fight to the tooth and yet, she can be helpful and good. I believe that all these characteristics belie a basic lack of confidence in herself, in her abilities, and in her innate worth as a human being. I feel that Elaine's defiance stems from the very fact that she is not sure that she has an intrinsic value and must constantly test those about her to have this re-established.

Her rudeness and insolence is perhaps the most striking thing about her. I have recorded ten examples of misbehavior. It is not as though she is unwittingly hostile—she realizes full-well the impact of her actions and seems to take great relish in hurting others. I feel this rudeness is indicative of insecurity; as on July 28, when we tried to discuss behavior with her she said, "you're against me." This was not the first time she had said things of that nature. She frequently says, "you don't like me" or "you favor Ruth." The more Elaine speaks in this vein the ruder she gets.

We had had a problem in the cabin with another girl who has honestly tried to reform—she has succeeded. When on August 4, the cabin discussed plans for "Secret Buddy Day" Elaine was the first to say, "I hope I don't get Audrey." This helps cabin unity *so* much! She is frequently, if not always, the center of disturbances. She almost invariably leads after-taps talking as on July 25, July 28, August 1, August 3, and August 4.

Whenever a counselor attempts to reason with her and help her with her behavior, she blows up—she can't take criticism of any kind. No matter what is suggested or how it is phrased, Elaine is on the defensive with a wise-crack or an insolent action. Examples of this may be found on July 27, July 28, August 2, August 5, August 6 and August 8. This surely seems to point to a person who feels the world is out to fight with her and she is waiting for it.

It is true that when she feels secure in her position or feels that no one is watching her, Elaine can be quite nice. On July 20, Elaine was friendly until she realized that it was not her "role" to be friendly in the cabin. She changed immediately. On August 2, she was helpful on our cookout. I think she felt she could make a worthwhile contribution to the group.

To sum up Elaine's behavior, the pattern of original disturbance and subsequent rudeness on being reprimanded stands out. It is apparent to me that Elaine lacks faith in herself and uses the guise of aggressiveness and belligerence to cover her own feelings of inadequacy. Perhaps if she were removed from this competitive situation, she would not be forced into this pattern. I sincerely hope that she can find the depth within herself to bear us through the crowded places.

CASE 3

Diary report

July 28   Eva grabbed the place next to me at breakfast.
Eva had a fight with Kay about the hat they were making together for the evening program.

July 29   Eva did her caper duty.
She reached for my hand to comfort her after Diane had sassed her.
She asked me to help her sweep the middle room floor.

July 30   Eva had a fight with Kay because Kay bounced her bed when she climbed up into the bunk above Eva's bed.

July 31   Eva ate dinner at the other table and had elbows on the table all through the meal. She also lifted the watermelon rind to her face. She raced me back to the cabin.

August 1   Eva came out after taps and asked me to help her change her bed in the morning while she did her caper so that she could get to her class on time.

August 2   Whined about having to remove her shorts at the time of rest hour.
Eva walked with me to dinner and sat at my table.
She watched me playing the piano after dinner.

August 3   I fixed her hair up into a bun for her. (She looked beautiful.) She thanked me.
Eva whined again about the shorts at rest hour.
She was playing a game in back of the cabin with her friends and cabin mates.

August 4   Eva whined because I couldn't fix her hair again for her. (She asked me between classes.)
She asked me if she could be hostess of the other table at dinner.
She was up after taps soaking her leg in water. (She had picked a scab open and the sore was bleeding quite freely.)
She came in during the rest hour and wanted me to start her on her knitting. I told her I'd start it for her after the rest hour—she whined that she wouldn't have anything to do during the rest hour unless I started it for her now. I repeated myself and she went back to her room.

August 6   Eva and I started her knitting. She sat on my bed for the majority of her free time and worked on her knitting.
She ran back to the cabin area after dinner to play categories.

August 7   I fixed her hair up in a bun for church. Also fixed Barb's hair, Eva felt hurt.

August 8   Eva had a date for co-rec and made a special effort to point him out to me when she saw him.
Eva and her date were having so much fun that they swam right out of the swimming area, and since I was life guarding, I had to go get her. (The waves, wind and her spirits were high.)

Case study

Eva's father is a merchant and her mother is a housewife and a student. She has one older sister and one older brother.

These facts are such as those you would find on a tree label in a nature trail:

Norway Maple
Acer platanoides
Aceraceae family
40 years old

The name, the family of trees, the age, etc., is before you. In a way Eva is a tree, a tree of life. I don't mean to imply that she stands as rigid as a tree, but she has parts within her personality which may be compared to the parts of a tree. The trunk of the tree has cortex, cambium, pith. Eva has a set of feelings which give her an outer personality and an inner personality. Her cortex—outer personality—is one which is appealing to her cabin mates and to young boys of her same age. She plays games with her cabin mates in her free time. She had a nice date for the co-rec day.

But Eva's tree of life is a bit more than standing bark. Under this cortex is some *soft tissue*. By this term I mean there is something more that you don't see at the first glance. This part of our tree of life is best shown in her cabin activities and in her attitude toward her superiors.

Eva is still very much of an individual. She doesn't think on the "group" level. She seeks to be noticed and specially treated. She satisfies this need by finding an adult comradeship with me. The diary indicates several times when she has come to me for comfort, sat on my bed, or fought for the seat next to me at the dining table.

Just as I am sitting here and writing this, she came into our front room during the rest hour and started to ask me a question. She stopped in the middle of her sentence and started admiring my craft project. From there she asked for a piece of pork rind which was sitting on my orange-crate-bed-side-table. I let her have a piece but requested that she stay in the front room to eat it. She did so, and then she returned to her bunk.

She receives attention through this coming to me and through whining. Several times I have requested on hot days that the girls remove their shorts during the rest hour. She appeared not to have heard me till I asked her separately to remove her shorts. Then she whined about it.

Another instance of this whining was when I fixed her hair for her. The first time it was a treat, something different. Then she took it for granted. I declined her request to fix it because of lack of time and she nearly cried. This generally happens when she doesn't agree or get her own way.

A more concrete instance concerning this is when she and Kay consistently quarrel. They can't seem to work together. The hat that was going to be for two ended up being for Eva when Kay had made special effort to get the reeds. The only solution was to suggest that Eva get the reeds for Kay's hat. This worked.

This attitude could possibly result from being the youngest child in the family. Perhaps decisions will waver if she whines long enough at home. In trying to help this girl overcome her problem, my counselor and I have been firm with our suggestions to her and concrete with our reasons for a decision. These plus a lot of patience are the only aids we have found.

For a child to whine seems such a little thing. And it is only a small scar in Eva's tree trunk. The bark will grow over this in time. And as the bark grows, so do the characteristics of this camper.

Eva's ambition is commendable. She's an A-1 student in most of her classes. She is creative in her cabin activity. I started her knitting a neck scarf for her father. She's progressing at a good speed for a beginner. She is also enthusiastic about games with her cabin mates.

Through this love of companionship and this ambition to find herself and working for recognition—though it be attention now—Eva is beginning to develop into quite a young lady. She still thinks about *herself, her* way, and *her* possessions, but a certain amount of this is expected in a ten year old girl. This self thought will dwindle as she begins to think more on a "group" level.

This tree of life is young. She has many growing seasons left. Each season a new branch will appear. These branches may resemble problems or characteristics within her personality. As the deer eat away or remove the lower branches of the pine tree, so

75

will society and mature thinking remove the problems of this camper. These two factors will also bring problems as well as take them away. But with a steady trunk and deeply set roots to support her branches, our tree of life will live on. Her bark is attractive; her cambium is marred with a few scars, but her life is ahead of her.

CASE 4

Two case studies on Walt follow. They were prepared during two consecutive summers by different counselors. Diary reports are omitted.

Case study A

Walt is a very good looking twelve year old, who is about five feet four inches tall with blond hair. He comes from a substantial family consisting of one sister and one brother.

For a boy of twelve, Walt shows a great amount of maturity and is also highly sensitive to problems around him. For example, one afternoon he noticed one of the campers in our cabin was not joining into the group because of extreme shyness, so Walt immediately proceeded to encourage this camper to join in on the fun. Throughout the first week of camp he continued to befriend others who were falling behind because of homesickness.

Walt has constantly maintained his position as a leader in the cabin group and has accepted responsibility with a great deal of pride. Whenever there is a sports activity underway, Walt is always in there plugging away and encouraging the others to do their best. Although during these games he makes mistakes and the others criticize him he takes it very good naturedly and never attempts to avenge himself by reversing the procedure when the others are at fault. He just smiles and says, 'that's alright'.

I find at times that Walt becomes very moody and degrades himself for not attaining the highest level of achievement of which he knows he is capable. Although he kicks himself all over he has never taken it out on the other campers or has even mentioned how he feels.

Walt is very easy to talk with and by talking to him alone I have been able to bolster his ego and give him more confidence. He is too quick to blame himself for something that is not his fault. One day I had some popcorn and I offered him some and he ate the whole bag. Afterwards, he was apologetic for doing so and exclaimed 'I'm sorry I'm a hog.'

He has a very even temperament and whenever he is mad he tries to calm down before speaking out against someone or something.

Walt was very much surprised when he was elected cabin representative to the Council. This really gave Walt the confidence in himself which he needed. As he expressed it to me, 'Gee! The guys really like me you know!'

As far as his social life is concerned he is developing quite rapidly, whenever he is describing one of his newest flames, the kids refer to him as *Dobbie Gillis and His Many Loves*.

In conclusion, Walt seems to be a well adjusted boy who is a little more mature than some of the others and is handling himself in such a way that he should, from all indications, develop into a fine musician and gentleman. He is in my estimation one of the finest examples of a camper that we have had.

Case study B

Walt is an extremely talented and intelligent camper with tremendous potential who has alternating cycles of elation and depression. When I entered cabin two, on Saturday of the fourth week, Walt was gay and ebullient, and bubbling about mutual friends. The next morning, however, Walt was depressed and commented, 'Camp is dumb. Everybody hates me.' After talking with Walt for a long time on the badminton court, I learned that Walt has been rejected by his schoolmates' social group, and consequently he has rejected his own peer group at camp. High school boys and girls have formed a substitute for friends of his own age level. This leads to frustration though, because Walt must spend most of his time living in a division from which he has exiled himself. In counseling we have attempted to tear down Walt's barrier to his campmates by providing him with pleasurable experiences with his peers. Moreover, since Walt can consciously control this cycle, we have kept him from returning to his depressed state by treating the first symptom of melancholy with a dash of praise, a dose of encouragement, and a chorus of laughter. This never fails! Walt is also beginning to express his emotions: he hollers more than he used to, he jumps on unsuspecting cabinmates, and he occasionally talks back to his counselors. Walt is obviously beginning to overcome his hypo-manic-depressiveness.

CASE 5

Case study on Ned (Diary report omitted)

In this my second case study, I find a completely different set of circumstances than those I encountered during the first four weeks. I moved from a cabin of boys who are eleven and twelve years of age, into a cabin of nine and ten year olds. Their behavior and actions are so unrelated to the first experiences that it took me sometime to adjust to them.

In this cabin, I encountered a camper who I feel needs help beyond what we or his parent has been able to give him. Ned is a very insecure and confused boy. But the blame for all this insecurity cannot be placed upon him alone. Without a father to guide him, it has been a period of bewilderment for Ned.

Ned is at the stage where a man's guidance is most important in his development and since he is not receiving that help he is attempting to find himself and is in effect drowning himself instead of coming to the surface. He does not respond to corrective counseling in any way, and maintains a high level of disobedience at all times. For example, one evening he was told to put on a clean shirt, and at line-up the dirty shirt still remained upon him. This attitude of refusing to do anything to improve his personal effects or his attitude towards the other campers is the only thing that is holding him back from becoming a number-one camper.

When Ned is guilty of making some kind of disturbance he immediately tries to push the blame off onto someone else. He has gone so far as to blame a boy for stealing an article of his, when the truth of the matter was that Ned had misplaced the article himself. I do realize that Ned is at the stage when it is normal for a boy to get into trouble and not respond to punishment or have it make a lasting impression on him; but he carries this point a little too far, there is absolutely nothing that can get through to him. He acts as though we were not even there.

Ned is very immature for his age as far as his actions go, but he is very bright as far as getting himself into trouble as well as pulling his fellow cabinmates in along with him. He seems to be a leader in the cabin but always in the wrong direction. Because of his warped sense of values and behavior he pulls the other campers behavior down along with his. If only he could be given some help to get him back on the path during this period when the development of his personality is so important, I feel Ned would be a great asset to the camp. He does have a high I.Q. and is capable of much more than he is putting out.

My experience in working with these two groups has not only enlarged my understanding of children, but of myself as well.

Charts

Charts that present a visual image of facts often are more forceful than the written word in showing strengths and weaknesses.

Charts come in many forms and are used for many purposes. Caper charts for cabin duty assignments, charts that show skill tests completed in swimming, and height and weight charts in the infirmary are but a few of the kinds used in summer camps. Counselors also need to be concerned with charts that provide information on the campers' interaction in the cabin group. Charts showing interaction of people are called sociograms.

One simple chart that requires some thinking and observation on the part of the counselor is one that depicts degree or strength and quality of leadership. Using three concentric circles, with the center circle denoting the greatest strength, the counselor places a symbol (number, letter, small circle, or small square) indicating a camper in the area that best indicates the strength of that particular camper's leadership.

The quality of leadership is represented by the color of the identification symbol. Green indicates positive leadership qualities; red indicates detrimental or negative leadership qualities. On occasion a camper's symbol may contain both red and green, indicating that the child leads or follows (depending upon the symbol's location within the concentric circles) both positively and negatively. The colors may be solid, half and half, or any other combination, representing various leadership qualities.

Further information can be depicted on the chart by connecting lines showing which camper seeks association with which other camper in his cabin. Sometimes clusters of associates will become apparent and the "ringleader" may be quickly spotted and directed into a force for good. Positions may shift daily and weekly and may move through complete cycles by the end of the camp season.

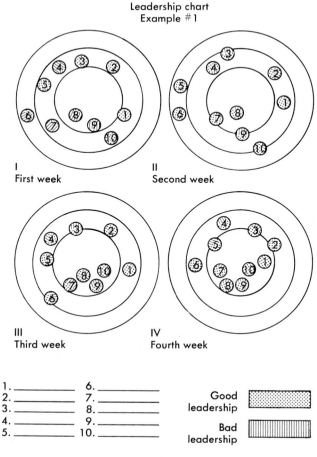

Leadership chart
Example #1

I
First week

II
Second week

III
Third week

IV
Fourth week

1. _____ 6. _____
2. _____ 7. _____
3. _____ 8. _____
4. _____ 9. _____
5. _____ 10. _____

Good leadership

Bad leadership

Some counselors have discovered that enlisting the campers' aid in making out the chart is an excellent means of achieving unification within the cabin group. The information on such a chart is not secretive as is the diary or case study. As a matter of fact, there would be no harm in posting the chart in the cabin for all to see. If the campers share in the determination of each other's strength and quality of leadership, as well as of their own, the technique may be just the right motivational force to encourage the "borderline" leader or the detrimental leader to strive for a more positive leadership position on the chart. What an accomplishment it would be for a camper to see his symbol change from red to green or move from the outside to the inner circle.

A leadership chart is an interesting technique for getting to know one another and requires honest and objective observation on the part of the counselor and campers. Its benefits are well worth the time required for its construction and use.

To do

Reviewing the application blank of a camper, recommendations, and the cumulative records kept in the camp file are methods of understanding the individual. The medical examination and the health records are also sources of information.

Access to these records is the privilege of the counselor, but the information is strictly confidential.

1. Diary report. Select a camper in your cabin whom you wish to observe carefully for four weeks. For the *first two weeks* keep a diary report on incidents that will help form a picture of this camper. Example: Jane made a pie, made her bed, or John punched George.

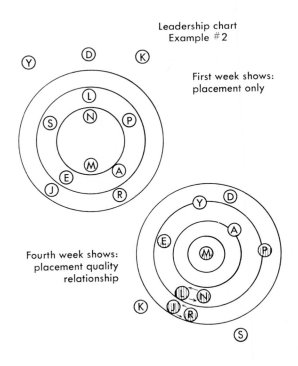

Leadership chart
Example #2

First week shows:
placement only

Fourth week shows:
placement quality
relationship

Black.
Negative leadership

79

Leadership chart
Example #3

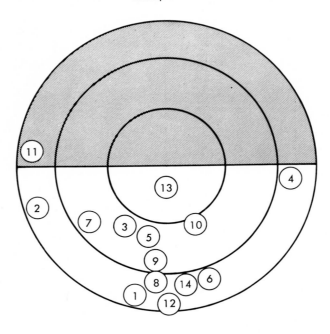

1._____	8._____
2._____	9._____
3._____	10._____
4._____	11._____
5._____	12._____
6._____	13._____
7._____	14._____

Shaded area represents
poor quality leadership

2. Case study. With the application blank data and the outline of events of your diary report, present your analysis of the camper and the reasons for his behavior. This is due at the end of the *third week*.

3. Chart. Draw three concentric circles. Using a symbol to represent each camper in your cabin, place the leader or leaders in your cabin in the *inner* circle. Use green to indicate good leadership and red to indicate the wrong kind of leadership. Group the followers in relative positions to the leaders so that the weakest are near the edge of the middle or outer circle, as the case may be. A well-knit cabin will find all cabinmates within or near the center circle. The wider the spread, the greater the divergence within the cabin group. It will give a picture of the quality and quantity of leadership. This is due the *Tuesday of the fourth week*.

4. *Repeat* the three assignments above during the last four weeks.

5. Thumbnail sketches done at different intervals will keep you aware of each camper's improvement or loss of ground. Write one for each camper at the close of the second day of camp.

6. Written observation. A good technique to help a counselor become aware of problems, understand them, and deal with them is to have each counselor write on a slip of paper at the beginning of each week a situation or problem they would like to have discussed. The supervisor or unit leader takes these, reads them, and turns them over to the direc-

Leadership chart
Example #4

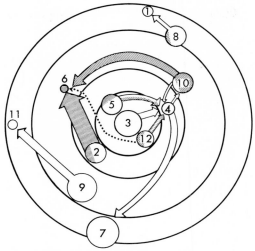

Size of circle shows amount of self-reliance
Distance from center shows amount of leadership
White coloring shows negative leadership ▭
Shaded coloring shows positive leadership ▨

Arrows show influence   Shaded shows negative ▨
                          White shows positive ▭

Thickness of arrows show amount of influence

1._____   7._____
2._____   8._____
3._____   9._____
4._____   10._____
5._____   11._____
6._____   12._____

tor of the camp or the person designated by the director to work with staff. Then the counselors, the supervisor, and the director have a meeting, which is conducted in an easy, informal, problem-solving atmosphere. The combined efforts of these people is a learning process for all concerned, as well as a means of alleviating the counselors' concerns.

> If a child lives with criticism, he learns to condemn.
> If a child lives with hostility, he learns to fight.
> If a child lives with fear, he learns to be apprehensive.
> If a child lives with pity, he learns to feel sorry for himself.
> If a child lives with ridicule, he learns to be shy.
> If a child lives with jealousy, he learns to feel guilty.
> If a child lives with tolerance, he learns to be patient.
> If a child lives with acceptance, he learns to like himself.
> If a child lives with recognition, he learns that it is good to have a goal.
> If a child lives with honesty, he learns what truth is.
> If a child lives with fairness, he learns justice.
> If a child lives with security, he learns to have faith in himself and those about him.
> If a child lives with friendliness, he learns that the world is a nice place in which to live.
>
> "Children Learn What They Live"
> Dorothy Law Nolte

Now, may I ask you, with what are your campers living?

Cabin counseling

Bring out the best in others

The dictionary defines the word technique as "the method or the details of procedure essential to expertness of execution in art or science"—and in counseling. Techniques are sometimes spoken of as tools of procedure. But, unlike the tools or instruments carried by the mechanic or the doctor, counselors' tools are not carried in boxes but in their heads.

Good camping is far more dependent upon *leadership* than it is upon equipment. The good leader should keep in mind that growing up means moving from dependence to independence and from authority to freedom. The cabin counselor should clearly understand the difference between command and leadership. *Command* implies *power over people*. *Leadership* implies *power over problems*.

Getting acquainted with all campers in the cabin

> *I will not wash my face,*
> *I will not comb my hair,*
> *I'll just pig about the place*
> *There's nobody to care.*
>
> *Anonymous*

1. Study camper's cumulative record.
2. Study parent information form or camper history sheet.
3. Camper-counselor dialogue.
   a. Make it casual, for example, a canoe ride, a walk in the woods.
   b. Make it informal. Let him do most of the talking.
   c. Keep it short.
   d. Its chief values are to assure the camper of your interest in him and that you do care; and to give you insight into the kind of person the camper is so that you may ascertain his needs, desires, and interests.
   e. Avoid giving the impression that you are setting a trap or trying to pry into his affairs.

Dealing with attitude and conduct

> *I do not like thee Dr. Fell.*
> *The reason why I can not tell.*
> *But this I know quite very well*
> *I do not like thee, Dr. Fell.*

The cabin is home and family for the campers. Unfriendly feelings toward cabinmates cannot be permitted to endure. It may be *a camper* or the *whole group* that needs help.

The most frequent problem areas for the camp counselor to deal with are slowness, isolationism, aggressiveness, cabin duties, rest hour, after taps, and conduct in the dining room.

Prevent conduct problems from arising by (1) showing sympathy and an understanding of problems; (2) having a genuine liking for campers; (3) showing no favoritism; (4) employing democratic methods but not hesitating to use authority when needed; (5) having faith in campers to accomplish tasks and to do the right thing; (6) being fair in decisions; (7) having a sense of humor; and (8) remembering that if campers are busy doing things that they enjoy doing, problems are not as likely to arise.

The following principles are helpful in handling behavior problems: (1) Reject the behavior but *not the child;* (2) All behavior is caused; (3) Watch out for the cold eye of the objectivist; (4) The *why* of the act is more important than the *act;* (5) Create a sense of responsibility (the third L—Liberty); (6) Moralizing does not help; (7) "Shut up" indicates that the counselor is desperate; and (8) Remember the age of the camper. He is not as old as you. Don't expect twenty-one-year-old behavior from a ten-year-old.

If punishment has to be used to reinforce the second L—Limits—do not let your own ego become involved. The punishment should follow the offense as soon as possible and be related to the act. Never use physical punishment. Remember, if you strike a turtle on his back, he will withdraw into his shell. Also remember that words can also be a terrible blow to a child. Keep cool. If the technique is to be deprivation, be sure the thing given up is not something that might prevent recurrences. If extra work duties are assigned, they should not be for the benefit of the counselor. The type and amount of punishment should be distributed fairly. The camper must be aware of the reasons for the punishment. Remember that sarcasm is rejection.

Homesickness is a frequent problem among campers. Factors causing it might be overattachment between camper and parent; attachment to chums back home; attachment to pets back home; lack of privacy in camp; lack of friends in camp; lack of skills; being unaccustomed to work; strangeness of night sounds at camp; or fear of being different. Symptoms include crying, strong attachments to others at camp, withdrawal, illness, moodiness, irritability and nervousness, strange eating habits, excessive letter writing, undue concern over lack of mail, telephoning, uncooperative behavior, temper tantrums, or other attention-seeking behavior.

There are a number of ways of treating homesickness. The counselor can help the camper find a friend; find interests and activities that appeal most to the camper and keep him purposefully busy; or get him to "sell" the camp to someone else. If hysteria behavior develops, ignore it. Hysteria must have an audience. Solicit help from the entire staff. Remind the camper to hold his head up—no one else can do it for him. Provide emotional first aid. In some instances the disturbance is serious enough that the child should be allowed to go home.

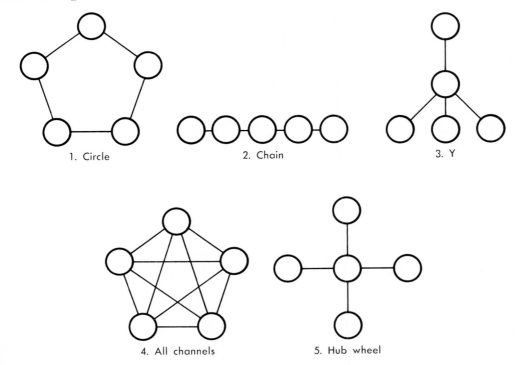

1. Circle   2. Chain   3. Y

4. All channels   5. Hub wheel

With all problems the counselor should make use of the referral system. Find out the resources available in the camp to help with various behavior problems.

Cabin group activities

The communication network in the cabin is of prime importance to the effective functioning of the group. Study the diagrams on p. 83 and determine when each might be useful or harmful in moving the group toward its goal.

Carrying out group projects

The following are suggested methods:

Positive suggestion. "How would you like to take an overnight?" "Don't you think so and so . . . ?"

Cooperation. The counselor is one of the group in developing an activity but does not act like a camper. "Yesterday I discovered a swell spot for a Council Ring for the cabin. Who wants to work with me to level it off and make seats?" Show a readiness to get your own hands dirty.

Faith. Express confidence in your group, and they will have it in you.

Approval. Give approval when the group does well. Criticize constructively when it does poorly. Commendation and criticism are delicate tools and require skill to use effectively. If the way the group does a thing is wrong, it would be better to suggest a way you think might be easier than to tell them it is wrong.

Poor conduct should not go unnoticed. If you hear swearing, for example, recognize it and do something about it. Otherwise, if the campers know you heard it, and you do not comment, you indicate approval. You may wish to speak to the offending camper privately.

Activities should grow out of the interests or desires of the campers and should not necessarily be those of the counselor.

Cabin activities

The counselor should anticipate a number of such activities, such as an overnight hike or sleep-out, building a council ring, organizing and conducting a devotional service, a nature treasure hunt, or planning and presenting a skit.

Table manners and dining room conduct

The yardstick of table manners includes appearance, posture, use of knife and fork, having food in mouth and talking at the same time, the sequence of eating, conversation—by whom and about what, leaving the table before the whole group leaves, and method of saying grace. The counselor can improve mealtime problems by setting a good example; discussing table manners, sharing food, and so on in the cabin prior to going to the dining room; assigning and rotating seating arrangements at tables; and presenting skits to show campers good and bad dining room behavior.

Mealtime provides an opportunity to check on other aspects of camper well-being. The counselor can check to see that the campers eat a balanced diet. The food is there, but does the child eat it? Behavior in the dining room can be a good clue of mental, emotional, and physical health. Loss of appetite can be early symptom of emotional or physical upset. The atmosphere in the dining room can affect appetite and digestion. Whether to say grace before meals will depend on the campers' attitudes. It is better to have a private grace than to have a mockery made of prayer.

Quietness after taps and during rest hour

For many first year counselors some of the most puzzling camper behavior occurs during rest hour and after taps. The ever present question seems to be, Just how much should I let my campers circumvent the rules without jeopardizing my control over them during rest hour or after taps?

Each camp has its own set of rules regulating what is expected of the campers during these two periods in the cabin. It would be presumptuous to indicate a set of rules that would be appropriate for all camps to follow since these rules should be based upon many factors, which vary from camp to camp. It is safe to say, however, that the rules pertaining to rest hour and taps will determine to a large extent the amount of difficulty the counselor has dealing with campers during these two periods.

Rules must be compatible with the characteristics of the age groups for whom they are intended. Sixteen-year-olds should not be expected to adhere to the same regulations that are necessary for nine- or ten-year-olds. During precamp the staff should discuss the rules and regulations for rest hour and taps and reach a general agreement concerning the extent to which these rules are to be enforced. Significant disagreements between counselors of a single age group over what is permitted and what is not can cause much unpleasantness for the campers and the counselors.

The following samples of the kinds of problems counselors encounter during rest hour and after taps could be discussed at staff meetings during precamp and at in-service training sessions during the camp season. Comments by the authors have been omitted so that the problems can be resolved according to individual camp philosophies.

Junior boys and girls (eight through eleven years)

1. "My cabin just will not be quiet at rest hour and after taps (and sometimes before reveille). I have tried everything I can think of—stories, races, singling out individuals, saying good night to each one individually, no store privileges—nothing works."

2. "Although camp rules state that the campers are to be silent before reveille, after taps, and during rest hour, they naturally try and see how much they are able to get away with. If I let them talk until they go to sleep on their own volition, the surrounding cabins are bothered by the din. What a mess!"

3. "I have a little girl in my cabin who often can't be quieted during rest hour and after taps. Yesterday, one of the other girls approached me with this problem. She said, 'Judy always keeps me awake during rest hour. When I tell a joke, even if it's funny, they tell me to shut up; but when Judy tells a joke, not even funny, everyone laughs.' Judy knows she is the leader and makes it very hard for me to discipline her. When I ask her to be quiet, she always has just one more joke. I've talked with her alone but so far it hasn't worked."

4. "Each day before rest hour and taps, my campers want me to promise that if the fellows in the next cabin make any noise, I will go over and shout at them. The other cabin doesn't make enough noise to be disturbing, but when one boy suggests this, all the others cheer in agreement."

5. "One girl complained of a stomachache after taps, but after a few kind words and a little affection, she felt fine again and was asleep in a jiffy when she got back in bed."

6. "After taps, one girl was seized with a coughing spell. This kept the other campers awake. Two finally got to sleep. The rest of the girls began talking and no amount of coaxing and pleading could quiet them. Finally, the cougher got to sleep but then was

taken with having nightmares and began to moan. The campers then began playing games. Finally, I got them to lie still without talking and soon after the cougher quit moaning. It seems as if the more the girls talked, the louder the girl moaned."

7. "What do you do with a child who simply is not tired and can't go to sleep?"

Intermediate boys and girls (twelve through fourteen plus)

8. "In my cabin I have two boys who are good friends and were in the same cabin last year. They both have an overabundance of energy and mischievousness and, therefore, make a disturbance during rest hour and after taps that the others are quick to follow. I think a private talk with these two would help solve the problem but I don't know exactly what should be said and how it should be handled."

9. "There is quite a bit of crying in our cabin. Generally someone is crying every night. One girl who is otherwise very mature gets quite upset about the health of her girl friend, and cries after receiving a letter from home. This is a recurring problem."

10. "What is a good way for enforcing quiet after taps or during rest hour without yelling at campers? If campers respect a counselor, will they be completely quiet during quiet periods? If not, how much noise is always to be expected? If campers do not respond to a logical explanation of the need for being quiet, should threats be resorted to?"

11. "In my cabin, one boy continually disturbs the others during rest period and taps with wild calls and talking. The problem, however, is that the boy never admits his guilt. For instance, he talks during rest hour and consequently draws a counselor into the room to shut him up. Then as soon as I get near his bed to ask him to keep quiet, he quickly takes the defensive and yells even before I say anything to him. He says he did not say a word and that everyone is picking on him. Thus, besides being a large distraction to the cabin in both his actions and his retorts, he lies with ease while looking me straight in the eye."

12. "Here is a technique I used in my cabin. The campers had been rather unruly the previous night after taps. Before rest period, I told them that they would not be allowed to leave their bunks or make any noise. Fifteen minutes of remaining flat on their backs instead of writing letters or reading was the punishment for making the first bit of noise, and fifteen more minutes for the subsequent noise. Sure enough, someone made a noise and I enforced the rule. All noise ended completely for the rest of the time."

Assuming that the rules regarding behavior during rest hour and after taps are compatible with the characteristics of the age group for whom they are intended, a few general statements regarding these periods in the day are applicable for all residential camps.

Children must have an "unwinding period" before they can be expected to climb on their bunks, remain quiet, and go to sleep. Relaxation experts tell us that human beings should have a complete change of pace about thirty minutes before they go to sleep and that our thoughts during this period of relaxation should not be centered upon what we have just been doing prior to bedtime. Sometimes, it is next to impossible to find time for this thirty-minute period at camp before taps, but counselors should see to it that the change in pace and thought of their campers is directed toward relaxation rather than excitement prior to taps.

To do

Make a list of techniques that you have read about, experienced, or observed being used in other cabins or from your visits to other camps.

1. Quietness after taps
   a.
   b.
   c.
   d.
   e.
2. Quietness during rest hour
   a.
   b.
   c.
   d.
   e.

"Housekeeping" and interpersonal interaction in the cabin

Camp provides many youngsters with their first experience of having to put aside personal wishes and desires to meet the social demands placed on individuals in a group living situation. The child can be untidy in his own room at home, and it is an imposition to no one but his parents. However, at camp he cannot enjoy the luxury of doing as he wishes with his belongings because it effects the living situation of all the other campers in the cabin. This is a hard lesson to learn for human beings of all ages; it is especially difficult for a child to learn.

It takes time, repetition, and an unlimited amount of patience to change a child's personal and social habits. The adult must be prepared to give a great deal of encouragement to the learner, and he must anticipate that there will be many setbacks before the desired goal is reached.

A group of counselors were asked to write down some of the puzzling problems they have encountered with respect to cabin duties. The following samples could have been written by any counselor at almost any camp in the United States. How would you proceed to resolve these problems if they were happening in your cabin?

1. Nine-year-olds. "The girls in the cabin simply will not pick up their things. During sweeping in the morning, this causes many little spats. Also, several lost items are causing some girls to complain."
2. Eleven-year-olds. "I have an eleven year old camper who, although small fits in with camp life well. However, she is extremely messy and often does not complete jobs. When directed, she does her work and cleans up. Her messiness is an everyday problem."
3. For all ages. "How can you make a person realize that he has a job to do and must do it?"
4. Twelve- and thirteen-year-olds. "The campers all try to do their assigned capers but they fail then to clean up their toiletries in the washroom, leave their shoes and bathing suits on the floor, etc. I have taken the articles which were left out of place and put them in a box. To redeem these articles, a camper must pay five cents. At the end of the camp term, this money will be used for the campers." (Authors' comments: The technique of charging campers money to gain back their personal belongings is an inappropriate way to encourage tidiness. It would be far better to demand that an act of kindness or a service to others be rendered to redeem an article.)
5. Twelve-year-olds. "My girls are twelve and I find that in order to get them to do anything, I seem to have to yell. Otherwise, I won't be heard and they won't do any-

thing." (Authors' comments. This counselor hasn't learned that it is a far better technique to lower the voice than to increase the volume to gain attention. The louder the adult speaks, the louder he must continue to speak to be heard.)

6. Thirteen-year-olds. "What can you say to a camper who is so careless in everything she does? She does not pick up her things after she uses them and then it is necessary to call her all over the cabin to pick up her things during capers."

7. For any age. "How do you make a person of eleven responsible for her duty? I have told her she is to do it, but then she goes out without doing it. I don't like to always be reminding her." (Authors' comments. Like it or not, the counselor had best keep reminding her until the child develops a desire to do her duty because it is her social responsibility to the others in the cabin. So long as it is done just because the counselor says so, the negligent behavior is not likely to be modified.)

As in all other behavioral situations, the example the counselor sets with his personal neatness will be reflected by the campers in their neatness, or lack of it, in the cabin. If the counselor's bunk is messy and if his personal belongings are in a state of confusion in his corner, he is in no position to expect that his campers will take a personal interest in their living habits.

In addition to fostering a desire for a neat and clean cabin, the counselor has many other duties to perform in the cabin that come under the heading of miscellaneous. Most of the situations described below involve habit formation and the acquisition of values. They are included with the hope that counselors and directors will find them to be good topics for discussion at staff meetings devoted to helping counselors solve the puzzle of normal camper behavior.

1. Fourteen-year-olds. "One camper has very poor manners. She fairly insults the other campers and never says please or thank you. The other campers complain about her rudeness. She does not know, I don't think, that she is doing wrong. However, she gets very sarcastic when corrected."

2. Ten-year-olds. "One of my campers has very bad grooming and will wear a shirt for a short while and it will be terribly dirty. She doesn't seem a bit concerned that she looks so messy."

3. For all ages. "How do you get girls to not sleep with their panties on under their pajamas? They will wear their panties for days without bothering to change them."

4. Thirteen-year-olds. "I have a girl who refuses to try to do anything with her hair. Most of the time, it flies straight up and out. I have managed to occasionally break through the barrier and then the hair has been decently combed. But on the whole, the situation is almost impossible."

5. For all ages. "Is it characteristic of twelve-year-olds that some girls are quite neat and some must be prodded to wash their faces?" (Authors' comment: Yes!)

6. Fourteen-year-olds. "The girls borrow things without asking for their use. Therefore, many campers have not received their belongings back and some are very upset about this."

7. For all ages. "Many of the girls show definite lack of respect when the flag is being raised or lowered by talking in a silly or loud voice, not paying attention, etc. The same thing happens during table grace and during our nightly devotions."

8. Junior boys. "At age eleven, some fights are to be expected. But when a certain party is constantly in one scrap after another, something must be wrong. Sam is always getting into fights. The boys tease him and call him names. Sam has a sharp temper and it flairs up easily. He often is whipped, and ends up crying, 'I'm going to kill him.' Most

of the boys in the cabin like Sam except for one strong enemy, Bill. Bill urges the boys to pick on Sam. How can I make Sam and Bill friends? I feel that Sam's problem would be solved if Bill would stop bothering him."

9. Any age. "All the girls in our cabin seem to pick on one girl. She is the scapegoat for all of their griping. It has gotten to the point where everything that goes wrong, is this girl's fault. I have tried to talk to the girls but they seem to feel justified in their accusations."

10. Any age. "One of my campers is always tired out. I've tried everything I can think of to perk her up, but the improvement has been slight." (Authors' comment. This is a referral problem. Camper should be sent to the medical staff.)

11. For any age. "How do you take care of campers who are play acting illness most of the time?"

12. For any age. "One camper won't keep her voice down. When I ask her to, she apologizes but is just as loud in a few seconds. She comes in with some little remark everytime something happens."

13. Girls of all ages. "The girls seem to enjoy hearing themselves talk. One girl constantly talks loudly and on trivial things. She needs no invitation to express her ideas. She just talks constantly."

14. All age levels. "One of the campers has suddenly started talking back to the counselor and cabin mates. No matter how much this camper is corrected, it seems to do no good. I overheard some of the other campers talking and they are all very mad at this camper. What type of punishment should I use? (Authors' comment. None. Punishment is not called for.)

15. All age levels. "Things seem to get lost very easily in our cabin. Hardly a day goes by that someone isn't missing money or some other belonging. It has gotten to the point where some of the campers are being accused of stealing."

Miscellaneous situations

1. Inspection of the cabin should be a twenty-four-hour job. No one really enjoys living in a "pig pen." Even the "pig might choose other surroundings if he had the chance." A cabin that is clean and neat *just* to pass inspection indicates that the *counselor* has not developed the habit of neatness. Besides inspection and Caper Charts, list other techniques for encouraging cleanliness and orderliness within the cabin.

   a.

   b.

   c.

   d.

   e.

2. List one contribution you have made to the adjustment of each camper in your cabin. Do not use names, use a symbol.

3. List ways in which the counselor can instill pride in "our home" with your campers.
   a.
   b.
   c.
   d.
   e.
4. What opportunities can you provide for the campers in a cabin to succeed *together?*
   a.
   b.
   c.
   d.
   e.
5. What ideas or activities did you or your campers come up with to "keep up morale" on a rainy day? If it has not rained yet, what do you plan to do when it does?
   a.
   b.
   c.
   d.
   e.
6. What activities did you carry out with your cabin group on cabin night during the first four weeks of camp?

7. What can be done within the first twenty-four hours after the camper arrives to help prevent homesickness and make adjustment to the new environment easier?

8. What did you do during precamp to get ready for your campers' arrival that would contribute toward the prevention of homesickness?

9. Describe how you handled one homesick camper (symptoms and treatment). If you did not have one in your cabin, report on one you observed in your division.

10. Counselors need imagination and need to help campers develop theirs. Give a thumbnail sketch of an incident in your cabin that demonstrates the use of imagination.

11. The counselor's notion of "fun" and the campers' notion of "fun" may be calendar years apart. Briefly describe one situation in which this discrepency was evident with you and your campers.

12. What is the difference between discipline and punishment?

Suggested readings

THE CAMP COUNSELOR

Benson, R., and Goldberg, J. A. *The Camp Counselor.* New York: McGraw-Hill Book Company, 1951.
Dimock, H. S., and Statten, J. *Talks to Counselors.* New York: Association Press, 1939.
Gardiner, G. L. *How You Can Get the Job You Want.* New York: Barnes and Noble Books, 1964.
Hammett, C. *A Camp Director Trains His Own Staff.* Martinsville, Indiana, American Camping Association.
Mitchell, A. V., and Crawford, I. B. *Camp Counseling,* Philadelphia: W. B. Saunders Company, 1961.
Ott, E. *So You Want To Be A Camp Counselor.* New York: Association Press, 1949.

UNDERSTANDING THE INDIVIDUAL

Allport, G. W. *Becoming.* New Haven, Conn.: Yale University Press, 1955.
Anderson, J. E. *Psychology of Development and Personal Adjustment.* New York: Henry Holt and Co., 1949.
Association for Supervision and Curriculum Development Yearbook. *Perceiving, Behaving, Becoming.* Washington, D.C.: The Association, 1962.
Cole L., and Hall I. N. *Psychology of Adolescence.* New York: Holt, Rinehart and Winston, Inc., 1970.
Coleman, J. *The Adolescent Society.* New York: Free Press, 1962.
Conger, J. J. *Adolescence and Youth: Psychological Development in a Changing World.* New York: Harper & Row, Publishers, 1973.
Coombs, A. W., and Snygg, D. *Individual Behavior.* New York: Harper & Row, Publishers, 1959.
Dixon, M. *Children Are Like That.* New York: The John Day Co., 1930.
Dyal, J., editor. *Readings in Psychology: Understanding Human Behavior.* New York: McGraw-Hill Book Company, 1962.
Evans, E. D., editor. *Adolescents: Readings in Behavior and Development.* Hinsdale, Ill.: Dryden Press, Inc., 1970.
Hamacher, D. E., editor. *The Self in Growth, Teaching and Learning.* Englewood Cliffs, N. J.: Prentice-Hall, Inc., 1965.
Harris, T. A. *I'm OK—You're OK.* New York: Harper & Row, Publishers, 1967.
Hartwig, M., and Myers, B. *Children Are Human Even at Camp.* Minneapolis, Minn.: Burgess Publishing Company, 1961.
Hauck, P. *The Rational Management of Children.* 2nd ed. Roslyn Heights, N. Y.: Libra Publishers, Inc., 1973.
Hutt, M. L., and Gibby, R. G. *The Child.* Boston: Allyn & Bacon, Inc., 1959.
Jenkins, G. G., Stracter, H. S., and Bauer, W. *These Are Your Children.* New York: Scott, Foresman and Company, 1966.
Lefrancosis, G. R. *Of Children: An Introduction to Child Development.* Belmont, Calif.: Wadsworth Publishing Co., 1973.
Maslow, A. H. *Toward a Psychology of Being.* New York: D. Van Nostrand Company, 1968.

Middlebrook, P. N. *Social Psychology and Modern Life*. New York: Alfred A. Knopf, Inc., 1974.

Moser, C. *Understanding Boys*. New York: Association Press, 1962.

Moser, C. *Understanding Girls*. New York: Association Press, 1962.

Mussen, P. H., Conger, J. J., and Kaghn, J. *Child Development and Personality*. 4th ed. New York: Harper & Row, Publishers, 1974.

Rafferty, M. *Suffer Little Children*. New York: Signet, 1963.

Rogers, D. *Adolescence: A Psychological Perspective*. Monterey, Calif.: Brooks Cole Publishing Company, 1972.

Rosenberg, M. *Society and the Adolescent Self Image*. Princeton, N. J.: University Press, 1965.

Schur, E. M. *Labeling Deviant Behavior: Its Sociological Implications*. New York: Harper & Row, Publishers, 1971.

Shostrom, E. *Freedom To Be*. Englewood Cliffs, N. J.: Prentice-Hall, Inc., 1972.

Spodek, B. *Early Childhood Education*. Englewood Cliffs, N. J.: Prentice-Hall, Inc. 1973.

Sullivan, H. S. *Conceptions of Modern Psychiatry*. Washington, D.C.: Will White Psychiatric Foundation, 1947.

COUNSELING

Blumenthal, L. H. *Group Work in Camping*. New York: Association Press, 1930.

Cartwright, D., and Zander, A. *Group Dynamics: Research and Theory*. New York: Harper & Row, Publishers, 1968.

Doherty, J. K. *Solving Camp Behavior Problems*. New York: Association Press, 1947.

Hartwig, M., and Myers, B. *Children ARE Human So the Counselors Are Puzzled*. Minneapolis, Minn.: Burgess Publishing Company, 1962.

Kinnamon, R., and Luehrs, A. F. *Camp Leadership Focus*. Dallas: CAMPAC, 1974.

Ledlie, J. A., and Holbein, F. W. *Camp Counselor's Manual*. New York: Association Press, 1963.

Mitchell, V., Crawford, I. B., and Robberson, J. D. *Camp Counseling*. 4th ed. Philadelphia: W.B. Saunders Company, 1970.

Northway, M. L., and Lowes, B. G. *The Camp Counselor's Book*. Minneapolis: Burgess Publishing Co., 1963.

Ross, M. G., and Hendry, C. *New Understandings of Leadership*. New York: Association Press, 1957.

Schmitt, P. A. Characteristics of Camp Counselors and Their Attitudes Toward Children. Master's dissertation, Woman's University, 1965.

Ure, E. *Fifty Cases For Camp Counselors*. New York: Association Press, 1947.

Van Krevelen, A. *Children In Groups: Psychology and the Summer Camp*. Monterey, Calif.: Brooks/Cole Publishing Company, 1972.

part IV

the program

This part of the workbook is intended to just *open* the door to some of the major areas of the camp program. Look at the program as a menu for a cookout.

Stick to principles.

Principles

The program in camp is a means of carrying out the objectives of the camp; therefore, every phase of camp life is part of the program, planned or unplanned. There are many general principles and factors that determine the camp program. List below as many of these principles and factors as you observe or read about.

Planning

The program is the real reason boys and girls enjoy camping. Whether the camps objectives are realized through its program will depend largely upon the skill with which the program is planned and carried out. Outline below basic fundamentals in program planning.

Activities

A good camp program is a balanced program of activities in various areas. List below specific areas that should be included in a camp program.

Evaluation

A difficult part of the camp program is evaluation by objectives. Summer camps, as well as educational and recreational agencies, have much to do to develop accurate and appropriate means of evaluating their programs. A plan for recording statistical data for evaluation of the program is essential. These records may be compiled from attendance figures for most activities; narrative group records; supervisory reports in particular areas of the program; skill tests, as in swimming and canoeing; observation; and from interviews with participants in activities.

Equipment and facilities

This section has been developed to make the counselor or CIT aware of good practice in the proper care, storage, and handling of equipment and to point out potential multiple use of facilities.

Buying equipment and deciding what is the best buy for the amount of money budgeted is a difficult job. Anyone who has had to do this literally shivers to see equipment misused. Much of the misuse is due to lack of education, but a great deal of misuse is sheer carelessness.

Use of equipment

List the situations you have observed where equipment has been misused.

Star the situations above where method of storage was the cause. An example would be table tennis paddles on the ground near the outdoor tables. In this case there was no agreed upon plan to leave them on the table or a rack. Nor was there any concern about leaving them outside all night unprotected. (It can rain.)

Can you name any items that could be made in camp and that would be reliable substitutes for a ready-made piece of equipment?

Storage of equipment

Look around you and in a few words describe your camp's method of handling the following:
1. Storage of balls
   Playfield type
   Tennis
   Table tennis (ping pong)
2. Storage of racquets
   Badminton
   Tennis
3. Storage of rainy day equipment
   Puzzles
   Games
   Books
4. Storage of campcraft
   Cooking utensils
   Plates, forks, spoons, knives
   Sharp knives, hatchets, axes
Draw a diagram of one method of storage for canoes.

Describe a method of storage for paddles and oars.

Describe what is important about the mooring of the following:
Rowboats

Lifeboats and emergency boats

Sailboats

Do you have any ideas that would allow for community storage of fishing equipment? Describe them briefly.

Inventory of equipment

Draw up an inventory sheet that could be turned in at the end of camp showing the need for repair, discard, and ordering of new equipment. This form could be used for all activities.

Sign out of equipment

Design a sign out form for the use of cookout and overnight equipment.

Multiple use of equipment

It takes ingenuity or inventive skill to see multiple use in side-by-side tennis courts or to adapt a smaller indoor space to greater activity use. Take a space in your situation and try to adapt it to greater use. Draw suggested permanent markings for the floor, wall, and so on.

List the activities you can visualize being conducted in this indoor space.

Using a hard surface space equivalent to the size of side-by-side tennis courts, list other activities that might be played on this area and sketch them on a plan drawn in the space below.

Waterfront set-up

1. The size of the swimming area is governed by two factors:

   a.

   b.

2. List the desirable qualities of a swimming area bottom:

   a.

   b.

   c.

   d.

3. The maximum depth of water in a swimming area varies according to the swimmers' experience. Indicate the appropriate maximum depth for the following groups.

   a. beginners or nonswimmers _____

   b. novice swimmers _____

   c. skilled swimmers _____

4. List methods of marking swimming area boundaries:

   a.

   b.

   c.

   d.

   e.

5. List lifesaving equipment that should be strategically placed in the swimming area.

   a. lifeboats equipped with _____

   b.

   c.

   d.

6. Draw a practical dock system showing width of sections and placement of ladders.

7. Describe a desirable diving structure.

Regulations and practices for a safe waterfront

1. Write a set of positive regulations to govern swimming in an organized camping situation.

2. Write a set of positive regulations to govern the safety of boating in an organized camping situation.

Arts and crafts equipment

Certain tools are necessary. What are they? How are they stored? Sketch a sample of each of the following:

1. Coping saw

2. Mallet

3. Modeler

4. Knife

5. Hand saw

6. Vise

7. Hand drill

8. Ballpeen hammer

9. Chisel

10. Tin shears

11. File

Special areas

1. Sketch a plan for a safe archery range or a safe rifle range.*

*The Children's Division of the Department of Social Welfare, State of Michigan, has a four-page set of Archery Safety Rules for Summer Camps drawn up by Myrtle K. Miller, Director of the Teela-Wooket Archery Camp, Roxbury, Vermont.

2. Sketch your idea of an ideal permanent campfire site.

3. Could the ideal camp have a quiet place in the out-of-doors? How could such a place be established?

Method of serving, or Presentation of activities

If the program is compared to a menu, the staff must decide how the food is going to be served—cafeteria or family style? Are any cook-outs scheduled? Will one person do all of the work? Will the staff get a chance to do some of it? It can be a shared event with everyone sharing the work. It might be on the beach, cafeteria style, with everyone sitting around a poncho spread out on the ground. A piece of driftwood, a few strands of grass, a beach flower, and a few stones and shells can make a decorative centerpiece with just plain old big flat stones with names written on them in charcoal for place cards. Watch out! Don't kick sand on the food!

Sports and games

And now we have come to the salad part of our menu—activities on land. New counselors indicate their concept of their ability to teach or direct certain activities when they fill out the camp application form. They rate their own competence. When they arrive at camp and see the facilities, talk with other counselors, and realize the emphasis put on an activity they had checked, sometimes they are shocked to find that they have overrated themselves on the application blank. During precamp, they may experience extreme disappointment, fear of being "found out", or may dread the remainder of the summer. An experienced sports teacher also may have a few uneasy moments if several counselors are teaching the same activity and there seem to be divergent points of view on methods of teaching a skill, as well as attitudes regarding the emphasis and time that is devoted to teaching methods.

Because such situations occur with practically every camp staff, a part of precamp time should be devoted to group meetings of counselors teaching specific activities. A short review of teaching techniques, rules, and so on is necessary for even the "old dogs" on the staff. If there is a counselor designated as "head" of an activity, he should know how many "skull sessions" will need to be held during precamp and during the course of the summer if the sports teachers are going to do the job that is expected of them. These sessions may have fancy names such as clinics or workshops, but regardless of the name they are actually study, sharing, and practice sessions.

Counselors should be expected to do good work, not only in their teaching but in all aspects of their jobs. Once in a while it does every adult good to stop and realize that there is dignity in work. Is there a greater satisfaction at the end of the day than the thought that during this day something was really well done? Young people, as well as some adults, undersell the dignity of good hard work because they do not know what work really is. Sometimes young counselors neglect to realize that camp counseling means *work*—real, honest-to-goodness hard work. They may have used camp counseling as a means to get to be in a certain section of the country, to be where friends are, for the fun *they* can have, for the tan they can acquire, or for a vacation. If they came to camp for any of these reasons, the director will need to double his efforts to help them realize the dignity of work. Work of any type requires a certain amount of dedication. A job done well stands out. Furthermore, it takes all sorts of well-done jobs to make a successful camp season. The work of nine men in a bucket brigade is lost if the tenth man drops the bucket. So it is that the counselor who teaches the camper a specific sport poorly may counteract a good job done by a camper's cabin counselor. The director must set the pace, the tone, and the level of work. What is more, he must require this level of excellence to be achieved in the counselor's work. If possible, the director should be the "listening ear" for the counselor who doesn't understand and whose questions turn into gripes if not answered fully. But most of all, if the director is to earn his title, he must *direct*. Directing means guidance, and there probably is not a human being anywhere who does not need guidance about something.

A person may feel ashamed of his work because he has done it poorly and knows that he could have done better or because he is trying to do something he truthfully does not like or believe in or because he knows he is not capable of doing it. The harm that such a person can do to others, especially to those younger than he, is formidable. Pride in work is a trait that can be acquired at camp if the director creates the proper tone during precamp by making the counselors feel free from the competition and pressures of the "outside world."

Educators are always busy developing ways to measure improvement in order to better motivate the learner. Testing, tournaments, and practice are just a few of the ways to further the acquisition of sports skills. Most teachers agree that getting the camper into the game situation as soon as possible is paramount. Isolated practice of skills should be kept to a minimum. If such practice is to be of value to the learner, it should closely resemble its use in the game. For example, the "bounce to yourself and hit" routine in tennis is never used in a tennis match but is necessary as a technique for teaching beginning players the forehand drive. The tennis teacher must quickly have the players progress from bouncing the ball to themselves to drills in which the ball moves *toward* the player. Good basic skills that give the learner greater satisfaction in a game are more valuable than a wide variety of fancy tactics that are ill-performed.

If the program and number of counselors allow for this kind of planning, classes can be geared to accommodate different skill levels that will help the learner move along at a greater speed. Directors should consider whether a more dedicated approach to a few well-learned activities would be more satisfactory to the campers than exposure to a wide range of activities poorly learned. Sports skills acquired by the young people of today, whether at camp, school, or country club, serve as the basis for leisure activities in the future. These skills should be at a high level and should motivate the individual to want to participate in the activity. It is a well-known fact that human beings will choose their leisure time activities on the basis of whether they receive satisfaction while engaged in the activity. They are more likely to find satisfaction through success than failure, and success in sports is dependent on skill.

Instructional films or film strips on many individual sports can be rented for use during precamp or during the camp season. Camps that emphasize sports would do well to own film strips for rainy day use. The films could also be used by the teaching staff for discussion and upgrading of instruction. When it rains, what happens to a sports class? Is it lost for the want of the "know how" to keep on teaching even though the group cannot be on the court with racquets in hand? Do we substitute another kind of activity? Go back to the cabin? Just sit around in the lodge? Are we lost for the lack of knowing what to do? Rules need to be discussed, along with care of equipment and what to look for in buying equipment. Many techniques can be practiced in limited space. What to do in a sports class on a rainy day at camp must be a part of precamp discussion periods.

Rainy days need not discourage campers or counselors. In the Egyptian myth, the miraculous phoenix was consumed in fire and rose in youthful freshness from its own ashes. And thus it is with a rainy day at camp. It can prove to be one of the most delightful days of the entire summer if the counselors exchange ideas and make plans during precamp as to what will transpire on those days during the camp session. Books and manuals on all sports are readily available. Sports magazines contain good and stimulating articles and provide excellent bulletin board material. Sporting goods companies often offer free-of-charge brochures on sports that include diagrams for making courts and fields. Staff members perhaps have attended concentrated training periods offered at national, regional, or state conventions. Information acquired there can be passed on to fellow teachers at camp.

Win by losing.

In camping the term for physical recreation—excluding waterfront—has been land sports, which consists of individual and team sports and games.

Recently, there has been strong feeling that the sport activities a young person can learn in school should not be repeated at camp. Camp should provide opportunities to do things that are not so easily done during the school year. List examples of such activities:

List the activities in your camp that have been taught to you in junior high or senior high school:

Camp objectives will determine the number and kind of activities offered, as will the terrain and facilities. The age group served also is a determining factor. List other factors affecting the selection of activities offered:

On rainy days the landsport activities are affected. Before other activities are substituted, what are some of the ways in which the sport activity can be carried on indoors?

A counselor becomes valuable when he is skillful enough at least one landsport skill to be able to teach it well without having questions about the rules, equipment, and facilities.

The counselor's performance quality need not be of championship caliber, but enthusiasm for the sport, and good performance in the game situation should be expected the person who accepts a teaching assignment. It goes without saying that previous teaching experience in the activity makes the person more valuable.

For the young person just starting in this field, the last sentence above presents a problem. *Experience.* How does a person get experience? There are several possibilities. Volunteer your services in your community during the school year. In cooperation with the physical education department, assist with the sport and observe it being played. Courses in recreational leadership that require service internship with a community agency provide valuable experience. Service of this kind warrants an evaluation that can be used as a reference with future employers.

Self-evaluation in sports

1. How do you rate your swimming skills?

2. List the sports in which you have had *some* training and in which with further training you feel you could and would like to assume some responsibility for teaching.

3. List the sports in which you have no training but which you would like to learn.

Perhaps you would like to file your activity notes in this section.

Games

Children are taught many things through games. The games selected should fit the age group for whom they are intended. Older children can tolerate a game intended for a younger age group more readily than younger children can tolerate games intended for older children. It should be possible to adapt the game to the space and equipment available, to allow for the entire group's participation, to teach it as simply as possible, and to arrange it in some order of activity tolerance. Persons teaching the game should know the game well, check equipment ahead of time and have it ready, and be sure boundary lines are well defined. When teaching, be brief but thorough and vary your method of presentation by using demonstrations, explanations, discussions, problem solving, and testing. Allow for questions *after* the first trial. If confusion occurs, stop and make corrections. Insist that participants observe the rules. Arrange game order so that there is easy transition from one game to another. Watch for signs of fatigue since injuries can occur. Allow "fun" noise but not "noise" noise.

List and draw at least five game formations.

Fill out the following chart:

Running and tag games	Formation and equipment	Age
1.		
2.		
3.		
4.		

Simple ball games		
1.		
2.		
3.		
4.		

Singing games		
1.		
2.		
3.		
4.		

Quiet games		
1.		
2.		
3.		
4.		

Relays		
1.		
2.		
3.		
4.		

Stunts	Formation and equipment	Age
1.		
2.		
3.		
4.		

Organized team games
1.
2.
3.
4.

Tournaments and awards

These forms of competition increase motivation. Many times an elementary class in an activity will end the season with a tournament. Persons not acquainted with different kinds of tournaments will find the old reliables, Round Robin and Elimination, to be useful standbys.

The chart upon which scores are kept has a lot to do with motivation and keeping a tournament alive. The age-old question of awards and rewards as yet has not been solved. Many camps have traditional, hand crafted awards that add to the spirit of each summer season. Others have a wide variety of expensive awards that are just as highly sought. The controversy over awards decreases if their use can be justified if they provide motivation, opportunities for persons of varying skill levels, and if the awards are not unduly expensive and time consuming.

Round Robin tournament. Every team plays *all* other teams. Teams could be divided into leagues, each league playing round robin and the winners of each league going into round robin play at the end. To determine the number of games that would be played in a Round Robin Tournament use the following formula:

$$\frac{\text{Number of teams} \times \text{number of teams} - 1}{2}$$

In a four team league it would be

$$\frac{4 \times 3}{2} = 6 \text{ games}$$

Elimination tournament. Such tournaments accommodate a large number of players in a short length of time. Teams are placed in brackets of two. When the number of teams is not a power of two, it is necessary to set up byes. If a team or individual draws a bye, they have no opponent for that round and must move on to the next. The tournament is better if the strongest players are kept apart for the greatest part of it. This process is called seeding.

Make a chart for a five-team Round Robin tournament. Do the same for an Elimination tournament for seven teams.

Ladder tournament. This is a continuous tournament since no one is eliminated. Each player may challenge the person directly above him or two above him (or three or four above depending on the number in the ladder). Players must be willing to accept challenges. If these are written or posted, there is less likelihood of disputes.

List other kinds of tournaments:

Make a tournament chart for some activity in your cabin or camp. These charts need not be for sports only. There are other areas where campers take turns.

Waterfront

What method of serving is most satisfactory for the favorite part of the menu? Well, each takes care of his own, but the servers should have set up the cafeteria line in a way that prevents catastrophes or disappointments. The beverage rounds out a meal just as the waterfront, with its swimming, diving, synchronized swimming, competitive swimming, lifesaving and water safety, water skiing, canoeing, boating, sailing, scuba diving, surfboard riding, and skin diving, rounds out the summer program. Bait casting should find its place somewhere along the shoreline and can easily be incorporated into the waterfront program. If casting is not possible, a pole, string, or hook and worm will meet the needs of everyone.

During precamp the skills of the waterfront staff should be checked. Those with weak skills should be encouraged to improve and to join a class with the campers. Endurance is an equally necessary asset. The various swimming strokes should be discussed, and agreement should be reached as to *the* way they will be taught at Camp X. If a camper is likely to have more than one swimming teacher during the course of the camp session (due perhaps to some sort of promotion system based on skill accomplishment), complete agreement must be reached among the waterfront staff as to the method and techniques for each stroke. Otherwise, the camper will be confused and hindered in his opportunity to progress to his capacity in swimming. It takes a wise, human engineer as head of waterfront activities to be able to steer the discussions of his staff in a constructive manner and to have the group arrive at a consensus of opinion without hurting or belittling the suggestions of anyone.

Waterfront rules and regulations pertaining to safety should be the same for campers and counselors. If the campers must pass a swimming test to be able to use the canoes, boats, sailboats, or water skis, then every member of the camp staff must pass the same test before using any of the equipment. If at all possible, time should be provided during the precamp session for staff members to go to the waterfront and pass the test if they anticipate using the equipment. Some staff members may not be able to swim well enough to pass such a test. These individuals should be encouraged to attend a swimming class during their free period.

Perhaps one of the most difficult points for the head of the waterfront to get across to his staff is the need of a security system of checking swimmers into and out of the water. We are assuming that all camp directors require their waterfronts to have such a system. No precaution is too bothersome if it means the difference between life and death. A counselor needs to see a drowning just once to be convinced of the need for security systems. It is the job of the waterfront director to convince his staff of this need without them having to witness the results of a drowning. Whether the system is in the form of a buddy board or a check-in written form is not important, as long as it gets the swimmers in and out of the water alive. A number of the aquatic references included at the end of Part IV suggest a variety of ways to develop safety procedures on a camp waterfront.

One counselor tells of a pond that served as the waterfront at one camp. The pond passed the safety test required by the state, a test that consisted of the inspector being able to see a white disc at a certain depth while no one was in the water. When the campers began swimming in it, the water became so agitated that the counselor could not see the bottom. Safety must be considered from more than one perspective.

Out of one hundred new applicants for the counseling positions, ninety indicated that they were able to teach swimming and boating (one or both). Of this ninety, seventy-five had *no* Red Cross rating or its equivalent. Unbelievable you say? Not if you work with college-age students. Some of them think they could lick the world if just given the opportunity, even though they have no idea as to how to go about it. The unbelievable part is the fact that some camp directors hire these people to do waterfront work. To put any of these unqualified young people on the waterfront in a teaching or guarding position is unfair to the counselor as an individual and to the campers who will unfortunately come under his supervision.

A well-run waterfront with good teachers will help the campers overcome fears associated with water and will create camper and counselor respect for the rules and regulations set up for the safety of everyone.

Set big goals for yourself.

Since most camps are situated on water it is not surprising that the waterfront plays a large part in camp programming. However, sometimes even older counselors do not realize that working on the waterfront may require a precious sacrifice: A person must be ready to lay down his life to save another. *If the person is qualified because he has been properly trained*, the chance of tragedy is greatly lessened, if not completely eliminated. A CIT program that includes training in this area not only benefits the individuals concerned but contributes toward filling the great demand for Water Safety Instructors. A qualified instructor can bring a group up to the point that a Red Cross staff member can come in and complete the training for the Water Safety Instructors rating. In some exceptional cases a person in the camp is qualified as a trainer and can therefore do the entire job.

Camp waterfronts must be flexible. A waterfront should try to include all phases of aquatic activity, particularly swimming and boating. Every year seems to bring some invention that can be used in or upon the water.

Waterfronts have *instructional* periods and *recreational* periods. As in other situations, familiarity with the characteristics of the specific age group determines the what, the why, and the how.

Waterfront staff

1. List personal qualifications and characteristics for swimming instructors:

2. List the director's training qualifications and duties:

3. List waterfront assistants' training qualifications and duties:

4. List the general counselor's duties and conduct guidelines on the waterfront:

Swimming

Length and time of swimming periods

1. The average length of each swimming period is _____.

2. _____ periods of swimming per day are standard in most organized camps.

3. One of these periods is in _____ and one is in _____.

4. A "morning dip" may be permitted for those _____ for a period of _____ minutes.

5. Evening swims are permissible on _____ provided _____. Time limits should range from _____ to _____ minutes.

6. Distance swims may be permitted if _____.

Check systems for swimming

1. Describe a check system for entering and leaving the water:

2. Describe a check system to be used while swimmers are in the water:

Instructions in swimming

The National Red Cross has gone through a period of redesign since 1972 and is now undergoing evaluation. Junior Life Saving no longer exists. The whole movement takes in a wider age range and encompasses a greater span of skills. One could say it is family oriented.

In Basic Water Safety one is taught how to save a life without necessarily being able to swim. A young person eight years old can learn to use ring buoys and extensions and can qualify without being a swimmer. For persons eleven years and older who have intermediate swimmer skills there are basic rescue techniques such as the use of head carry or use of wrist on a passive victim.

Advanced Life Saving cards can be obtained by an individual aged fifteen or over in what was the Senior Life Saving Course, which required learning escapes and releases as well as life guarding practices at a beach.

Water Safety Instructors receive training in first aid and cardiac-pulmonary resuscitation. People seventeen and older can train for the Water Safety Instructor after testing by a Water Safety Trainer, a person of experience who is recommended by the area office. A limited number of people receive the rating of Trainer.

Record your present skill level and state what you would like to accomplish this summer. Evaluate your progress at the end of the summer.

File your materials on instruction in swimming after this page.

Recreational swimming

Water games or stunts. Briefly describe three examples for each of the following classifications:

1. Beginners

2. Advanced

3. Corecreational swim activities

Ballet formations. Draw stick figures to show three formations.

Small craft

The American National Red Cross conducts schools throughout the country for small craft instruction. If the facilities warrant it, occasionally there will be instruction at an aquatic school. A qualified person can earn an instructor's rating in small craft. There are special manuals for boating, canoeing, and sailing.

File your notes on any of the above after this page.

Social recreation

Take the unwanted jobs.

The word social means friendly. When applied to society, it means groups or communities. Therefore social recreation means any form of friendly group recreation. Parties, dances, campfires, games, singing, story telling, and rainy day activities can come under this classification.

Parties

Any party requires careful planning. The leadership is important. The positions usually are chairman, master of ceremonies, assistants familiar with plan, song leader, square dancing caller, judges, hosts and hostesses, piano player, and so on. These people must be reliable, friendly, and have the ability to work with people.

Leader selection requires careful thought. Should they be appointed, elected, or volunteers? Is it out of place for a person to *want* to do something? Have the group concerned close their eyes and then ask all those interested in being chairperson raise their hands. Place these names on the board for the group to see. After a "thinking period" have everyone close their eyes again and vote. If time allows, all those interested in the position could write out a petition containing their ideas and suggestions for the event. The group would then be better informed but would vote with eyes closed or by ballot.

After a chairman is selected, try a steering committee or planning committee of two or three more people. This group would meet and then recommend to the total group the number of committees they feel necessary to complete the event. Here again, people can sign up for committees on which they would like to work. Once these groups have been formed, each group could elect its chairman.

The following steps in preparty planning are suggested:

1. Obtain a central committee. Each member of the central committee should have a definite responsibility. The central committee could decide on all important matters such as time, place, theme, and so on.
2. Build the entire party around a theme, such as a birthday, season of year, a place, fad, and so on.
3. Invitations and publicity should follow the theme.
4. Decorations should follow the theme and be simple.
5. Properties and equipment would include tables, chairs, piano, stands, mikes, and so on.
6. Costumes can be used to create atmosphere.
7. Prizes should be simple, inexpensive, and appropriate.
8. Refreshments are always a welcome feature. They should be simple and in keeping with the party theme.
9. The clean-up committee often makes or breaks the chances of having other parties or privileges.
10. Evaluate the event.
11. Write a report for future use.

Party suggestions

1. Start the party when the first guests arrive.
2. Use individual and group mixers, such as get-acquainted games, conversational methods, identification games, or a grand march.
3. Provide for an easy transition from one activity to another.
4. Arrange for diverse activities. Examples are quiet games, dramatic stunts, active games, musical mixers, relays, quizzes, dancing (social and square), entertainment, small equipment play, stunts, tricks and magic, and group singing.

5. Provide simple refreshments.

6. Terminate the party while the group still has enthusiasm.

Other types of parties might be a sports day, including landsports, a swim, a picnic supper, and campfire; mixed swim days; or campfires.

Outline a plan for a party.

Dancing

Dancing as a form of social recreation has found a place in most summer camp programs. The type of dance may be somewhat dependent on whether it is a girl's camp, boy's camp, or coeducational camp. Although a specialist is needed to call square dances, teach folk dances, or teach some of the more complicated variations in social dance, many counselors with little or no previous training in dance can make a contribution to an evening of dance activity. In a coeducational camp it is absolutely essential that men counselors assume an equal share of the responsibility in calling and teaching. The value of joint planning between men's and women's recreation staffs cannot be overemphasized. A successful evening of dancing *will not* just happen. Its success is dependent upon careful preplanning and the ability of the staff to rise to the occasion during the evening.

Ice breakers and mixers

Regardless of the type of dancing that is to be emphasized, *all* programs should begin with a few ice breakers or mixers. These dances should require little or no dance skill, and the first ones should not require a partner. In the space provided indicate four ice breakers or mixers. Example:

Name of dance: Musical Madness.

Beginning formation: Single circle, no partner.

Basic instructions: One long blast from whistle indicates single circle moving clockwise. Short blasts from whistle, dancers form smaller circles. The number of short whistle blasts dictates the number of dancers in small circles. Dancers left out of small circles meet in middle of room and try to combine to form required number but always return to large single circle. Repeat several times, varying numbers for small circles. If next dance requires a certain number of people, end with that number in small circles.

1. Name of dance:
   Beginning formation:
   Basic instructions:

2. Name of dance:
   Beginning formation:
   Basic instructions:

3. Name of dance:
   Beginning formation:
   Basic instructions:

4. Name of dance:
   Beginning formation:
   Basic instructions:

Square dance

Square dancing certainly needs no champion today. It has captured the fancy of youngsters and oldsters alike. "Live" callers are much preferred to using records with calls on them. Learning to call square dances necessitates a great deal of practice to perfect a feeling for phrasing and rhythm in the music and to memorize the calls. Dance patterns vary, but generally there are three parts included in all square dances: introduction, figure, and ending. Using the references given at the end of Part IV, record in the space provided an introduction, figure, and ending that you might combine if you were required to call a square dance.

A Virginia Reel is usually included sometime during an evening of square dancing and with just a little practice most anyone can lead one. Indicate in the space provided the sequence of figures you would call for a Virginia Reel.

Folk dance

Folk dancing involves the position, formation, and folk dance steps of different countries. Here again, young and old enjoy the exhuberance that builds as they dance. The polkas, schottisches, two-steps, and waltzes found in international folk dances certainly have a place in camp programs. The great need for a better understanding of our world neighbors can be partially met through learning the dances of other countries. Such experience at camp can help develop an appreciation of the vigorous Russian dances, the formal English dances, or the strenuous, fun-filled Scandinavian dances and thus help campers become better world citizens. The pageantry of International Nights or folk festivals, replete with costumes, deserves a place in program planning for summer camps.

Social dance

In coeducational camps there are many opportunities to use and teach social dancing. Besides providing an evening of fun, social dancing provides an opportunity to teach the simple rudiments of manners. The success of an evening of social dancing depends upon the boys' ability to lead and execute the steps adequately and the girls' ability to follow well enough to be in demand when partners are changed.

Men and women counselors and program directors should take time prior to the dance to teach their campers the basic step patterns of some of the simple ballroom steps. It is false to assume that each boy and girl in the camp is well versed in the art of executing basic dance steps. There is nothing more painful and frustrating for a boy or girl than to be embarrassed on a dance floor because of a lack of dance skill. Time spent in predance instruction is time well spent when the counselors observe that their campers are confident and well mannered at the dance.

In the space provided record the basic steps for the following:

1. Fox trot

2. Waltz

3. Rhumba

Add three of the latest steps you know.

Music

The child has physical, ethical, intellectual, and aesthetic potential. Education must therefore assume responsibility for developing these potentials.

A music school dean challenges the type of musical materials we use in camp. He thinks songs like "Do your ears hang low" should not have a prominent place in our repertoire. If we think about it, there are some beautiful camp songs to be taught.

Singing

No one would question the place of singing in camp. Many times it is spontaneous and many times planned. The nonmusic major can equip himself with enough aids to be helpful in a "singing situation."

1. List the places where group singing usually occurs.

2. Draw the tempo directions for 2/4, 3/4, 4/4, and 6/8 time.

3. As a song leader, how would you give your group directions to do the following:

   a. hold a long tone

   b. sing forcefully

   c. sing quietly

   d. stress a beat

4. Name ten songs and classify them by type.

5. List the titles of camp songs you hear during the season that are "educationally beauti-ful." (We usually put together a list of songs with the words, which you contribute. This will be distributed the last week in camp.)

Instruments

Campers often bring their own instruments to camp. Instruments can be made. A great deal of music appreciation can be fostered depending on *how* the topic is developed. There are many good records that can be used to augment the teaching.

Interesting sounds can be made by combining different media, for example, a washboard and thimbles. Invent some combinations and list them:

Campfire programs

The usefulness of campfires is not limited to overnights and trips. They can also be used in a very powerful way within camp. Campfires can have a quieting effect, they can be exciting, they can provide the focal point for a group sing, a story, or a ritual. All of them should be planned. They can be planned by the campers, staff, or a combination of both. All the campers should have an opportunity sometime during the summer to work on one of the fire programs. Junior campers are capable of putting adults to shame in their ability to recognize the qualities of a "good person." They can even tell you how to become one. Vesper or devotional events often stem from the idea of a campfire.

Whatever the name the program takes, it can be worked into an annual and much looked forward to event. Skits around a fire are difficult to do because of staging, sound, and visibility problems and possible danger. The length of time depends upon the type of event; again the age group being served dictates the length of the event.

To do

Outline plans for a campfire program for campers.

Storytelling

Since stories are really a form of entertainment, there are several factors to consider before attempting to be a storyteller.
1. List the occasions at your camp when storytelling could become a *regular* part of the program.

2. Are there times when storytelling is not planned but is used as a substitute activity or for a specific purpose? What are these?

In choosing a story determine whether it is appropriate for the age level, it is appropriate for the occasion, and it fits the time allowed for telling. Be familiar with the story, have all characters clearly in mind, know the action sequence perfectly, eliminate unimportant sequences, and practice.

When telling the story be in the best possible position for your audience. This will vary with different age groups. Wait for attentiveness, watch the faces, and establish eye contact. Use your voice expressively, speaking clearly and slowly. Proceed to the climax, and have a clear cut ending.

List the stories you have heard told within the camp program during a two week interval. Indicate the occasions on which they were told.

As alternatives to the classic favorites, current literature contains many good and interesting stories. Among most groups of people there will be a common thread of familiarity with childhood classics that they are anxious to pass on to others. Name a few of these classics.

Dramatics

Informal skits and stunts are forms of dramatics. The close relationship of this area to storytelling should not be overlooked. The cabin counselor may need to delve into informal dramatics on many scheduled and unscheduled occasions.

The serious production of a play, including playwriting, staging, costuming, and advertising, is usually in the hands of a skilled and trained person. One can learn many things if one works along as a volunteer on a production.

Other forms of dramatics are imaginative play (pretending), story plays, impromptu plays, pantomine, miniature theaters, puppets, shadow plays, tableaux, pageants, and ceremonies.

Campcraft

Start from where you are.

In its broadest sense campcraft includes every activity and skill associated with camping. For the sake of convenience, it has come to have a somewhat more restricted meaning. The term commonly includes hiking, fire-building, outdoor cooking, trips using various means of transportation, pioneering, and general woodcraft lore, including the use of knife, axe, compass, map, trail laying and following, weather signs, and so on. Campcraft is a "doing thing," and you will learn only as you practice some of the suggestions given you.

Outdoor cooking

Good outdoor cooking depends upon proper preparation and planning in advance to make sure you will have everything that you need and that every member of the group has a share in the tasks.

List factors to consider in planning your food supply:

Make a list of items you will need to prepare a breakfast for twelve campers:
Menu:

Supplies:

Utensils:

Divide the group of twelve into committees and give each a share in the tasks to be done. List general hints for packing food and utensils:

Cooking and living arrangements should be as attractive and convenient as possible. Describe or draw and label a plan for a well arranged breakfast. Include fireplace, wood-pile, and so on.

Improvisation is important in the preparation of food.
1. Give hints for cooking meat.
   a.
   b.
   c.
2. Give three ways of preparing eggs. (One without using a utensil)
   a.
   b.
   c.
3. Write two recipes for one-pot meals.

4. Make four suggestions for nonutensil dishes.
   a.
   b.
   c.
   d.

   Proper clean-up is an essential part of camping. (One southerner prefers to call it Restoration!) Make suggestions for the following items:

1. Garbage

2. Pans and kettles

3. Eating utensils

4. Papers, boxes, and so on

5. Tin cans

6. Unused food

7. Fire

Swap page

Did you know?

A pint's a pound the world round.

Rule of thumb
  1 pinch between thumb and finger is ¹/₆ teaspoon
  1 pinch between thumb and two fingers is ¹/₂ teaspoon
  1 pinch between thumb and three fingers is 1 rounded teaspoon
  1 fistful, slightly rounded is ¹/₂ cup
  1 double fistful, all that both cupped hands will hold, is 2 cups, or 1 pint
  Butter the size of a walnut is 1 tablespoon
  1 level saucerful is ³/₄ cup
  1 paper plate is 3 cups
Dry measure
  8 quarts is 1 peck
  4 pecks is 1 bushel
Liquid measure
  1 fluid ounce is 2 tablespoons
  8 fluid ounces is 1 cup
  16 fluid ounces is 1 pint
  32 fluid ounces is 1 quart
  4 quarts is one gallon
Capacity of cans
  No. 1 tall = 2 cups
  No. 3 = 4 cups
  No. 5 = 7 cups
  No. 10 = 12 cups
  Without a clock tick off the seconds: "One chipmunk, two chipmunk, three chipmunk"
—up to "sixty chipmunk," or one minute. Add other counting techniques:

Fire building *

The kind of fire that you make depends upon the variety of wood and kindling at hand, the weather conditions, the immediate surroundings, and the intended use for the fire (heat, cooking). Observe the following precautions when selecting a site for your fire: (1) Build it in a clear, open space; (2) Clear away all leaves and rubbish, in a radius of five feet around fire; (3) Build only small fire; (4) Choose a spot on water or upon rocks, if possible—never against or under a tree; (5) Never leave fire unattended; (6) Extinguish with water first, then cover with dirt or sand. "Practically out" will not do; the fire must be *out*.

Fire building materials

Tinder is the kind of material that will catch easily from a lighted match. List materials that can be used for tinder:

---

*Materials on firebuilding and woodcraft contributed by Florence Petersen.

Kindling is next in size and should be graduated in size from twigs just a little bigger than tinder to pieces as thick as a thumb or larger. Soft wood makes the best kindling. List woods that can be used for kindling.

Fuel or firewood is the wood that really makes your fire. It should vary from branches of good size to logs at least a foot long. The amount needed depends on use of fire. List and be able to identify at least three good firewoods:

Starting a fire

Have plenty of air with a good draft from bottom to top. At the same time the fire must be compact enough that there are no big air holes. Start with a good supply of tinder. Pile it against an upright stick tepee fashion, leaving a small opening at the base where a lighted match can be put. Have *plenty* of small twigs at hand, and light the fire with the wind at your back. Since the flame will move upward, light the tinder from underneath. When it is well ablaze, put on additional wood, slowly increasing the size of the fire and building the desired shape of fire.

Kinds of fires

Draw examples of the following kinds of fires and state the purpose of each:
1. Wigwam (tepee)

2. Hunter-trapper

3. Crisscross or log cabin

4. Trench

5. Reflector

If you were camping on an extremely cold night and needed fire for warmth, describe the type of fire needed and the placement of bed for warmth.

Woodcraft

Use of knife

DO (1) Whittle or cut *away* from the body.
     (2) Keep finger behind blade.
     (3) Keep the knife clean.
     (4) Have a sharp blade.
DON'T (1) Carry an open knife in your hand.
     (2) Run the blade of the knife into the ground to clean it—this dulls it.
     (3) Pry things open with the blade or use it as a screwdriver
     (4) Hammer with the blade of the knife.

Axes and Hatchets

DO (1) Carry an axe or hatchet in a sheath.
     (2) When carrying an axe or hatchet, have hand close to head of axe with blade down.
     (3) Carry loosely enough to drop quickly if you should trip.
     (4) Be sure that head of axe or hatchet is on firmly.
DON'T (1) Swing axe near people.
     (2) Hold a stick of wood in one hand and chop with the other.

Hikes and trips

Out-of-camp hikes and trips are an important means of providing new and exciting experiences. They are of value, too, in that hiking skills are relatively simple to attain. All types of campers can participate in the activity on an equal basis. The beauties of nature are much easier to talk about when everyone is in the midst of them. There is nothing like a hike to give the counselor an opportunity to learn the temperament of the campers, how they cooperate, and how well they can modify their own likes and dislikes and live with the group. A hike or trip also gives the counselor an excellent opportunity to show the group that he is "one of them" and to be accepted by them by doing his share, maintaining an even, patient, and cheery good humor that may turn trying situations into humorous ones.

General hints

1. Careful planning is essential and should be done by the whole group. Planning includes where to go, what to take, when to return, and what responsibilities each

member is to assume. On certain trips a check by a nurse or doctor is advisable. Individuals who are not in good physical condition should not be allowed to go.

2. Check each camper before departing to see that he is properly equipped. Too much is as bad as not enough.

3. Rests should be planned for and taken as frequently as necessary. Hikers and trippers should not return to camp exhausted. Trips that are too long and exhaustive defeat their purpose.

4. Permission should be secured in advance for use of property. No fires should be built or wood cut without permission from the owner or director. Express an appreciation for the use of property and privileges granted.

5. Watch fires carefully. Put out fires entirely by using water.

6. Avoid drinking water from springs or wells unless they are known to be safe.

7. Clean up cans and other refuse before leaving the site. Leave it cleaner than you found it.

8. Give careful attention to toilet accommodations.

9. Check all equipment before leaving the site to see that you have it all and that every member has his share to carry home.

10. If swimming is part of the program, it should be adequately supervised. The counselor should be a Red Cross Water Safety Instructor and the swimming place should be tested and approved.

Kinds of hikes and trips

Hikes are taken for a number of reasons: star study, geology, fishing, gypsying, visiting sawmills, beaver dams, and historical sites, bird walks, photography, or treasure hunts. Trips might be hiking trips, horseback trips, backpack trips, or mountain climbing expeditions. The method of travel might be a sailing boat, canoe, motor boat, truck, pack mules, or covered wagon.

Hiking hints

1. Know how to walk. Cover the most ground with the least effort. Point toes straight ahead, and come down lightly on your heels.

2. Speed in walking should be governed by terrain. Adapt your pace to the distance you intend to travel and the pack you are carrying. The pace should fit the slowest member of your group. Short rests at reasonable intervals are better than long rests at long intervals.

3. Proper care of feet is important. Wear comfortable, well fitting, broken-in shoes with flat heels and square toes. Rubber-soled sneakers are not generally good for hiking. Woolen socks are usually better than cotton ones because they absorb perspiration.

4. For safety's sake on the highway, walk single file on the left-hand side of the road, facing traffic. Watch for cars, and get off the road when you see one coming. Cross country, on trails or off, watch your step. Always use common sense.

5. Clothing should be strong enough to protect you from snags, rocks and brush. It should be selected for the place and the weather and should fit loosely enough for easy movement of arms and legs.

Overnight or longer trips

Sleeping comfort and sanitation require special attention on longer trips. A sleeping bag is preferred by many and is comfortable and warm for outdoor sleeping. If your campers do not have one, they need not be deprived of the fun and comfort of sleeping out. If made properly, a blanket bed will be comfortable and warm. There are several ways to properly make a blanket bed, which will be demonstrated and practiced.

The following are some general hints:

1. Leave sheets and pillows at home. Use neatly folded clothes and sweaters for a pillow. Doing this will also insure having dry clothes.
2. Use a ground cloth underneath you to protect against dampness and cold from the ground.
3. Have as many or more thicknesses of blankets under you as you have over you.
4. For two or three nights in wooded country, you can collect dead leaves, boughs, or grass (bracken, and so on). Put your ground cloth on top of them or around them to form a mattress.
5. Bedding should be aired and thoroughly dried during the day. Moisture given off by the body during the night is absorbed by the bedding. Bedding is much warmer if it is dry.

The following are essential sanitation practices:

1. Burn all papers, and burn or bury garbage away from campsite. Egg shells and citrus fruit peels do not burn in an ordinary campfire.
2. Dish water should be disposed of by digging a trench some distance from the campsite. It should be sprinkled with lime or wood ashes every day and covered over when you break camp.
3. The construction of a latrine is a must for overnight camping. It should be constructed in an isolated spot—preferably a hillside—surrounded with brush and trees and some distance from the campsite. For methods of construction see *The Outdoor Book* by Camp Fire Girls, Inc. or *The Junior Book of Camping and Woodcraft* by Mason. Waste material should be covered each time by throwing loose dirt in the hole. Before leaving camp cover the hole completely with dirt so no trace is obvious. A forked stick can be used to hold toilet paper. It may be protected against moisture by covering with a tin can that has both ends removed. Lime or wood ashes sprinkled in and around the hole help to eliminate odors.

For practice, provide the necessary information for canoe trips:

1. Camper requirements for day trips

2. Camper requirements for overnight or longer

3. Loading canoes

4. Camp site requirements

5. Necessary supplies for trips, including trip essentials and campers' required list

6. Pitching camp

7. Returning to base camp

Trail blazing

Trail blazing may be used to stimulate the interest and imagination of campers on hikes or trips. It is also a means of making a trail for others who may wish to follow.

Half the group starts off one-half hour or so before the remainder of the group to blaze or mark the trail. Various preferred blazes that may be used are illustrated below. Chipping or marking trees or leaving a blaze of paper are the techniques of poor hikers. Sticks and stones are often used as markers for trails. Tied grasses are very apt to be disturbed and send the trail seeker in the wrong direction.

1. How would you indicate a right turn with stones?

2. How would you indicate the appropriate direction with sticks?

Nature (outdoor education)

NATURE

And God stepped out on space,
And He looked around and said:
I'm lonely–
I'll make me a world.

from the "Creation"
James Weldon Johnson

Nature is the world and all that is in it except what man has made himself. Children are very curious and very much aware of the world around them. This interest needs to be kept alive and not dulled, as it can be by forcing nature study upon children as work. The counselor needs to be aware of that important "teachable moment" and to take advantage of it. The controversy over Rachel Carson's *Silent Spring* is rekindled every once in a while when some group tries to discredit her statements about the effects of insecticides on nature. Regardless of its date and which side of the argument the reader chooses to take, this book is a must for everyone in camping. There is a wealth of knowledge in the book about the things that surround us in nature—things many of us perhaps would never know.

Camp directors and counselors should know as much as possible about the natural setting of their camp. There is a heritage about each camp site that needs to be passed on to the younger generation. At camp there is an opportunity to take time to look about us, time to learn something, and time to share it with the campers. Days and nights at camp furnish marvelous opportunities to drink in all the wonders of nature. Memories can be stored up for the dark winter days when we reminisce in front of the fire or over a cup of coffee. During precamp and throughout the summer, everyone must take time to notice the things of nature. It is really the very heart of camp programming. We must continue to learn about nature and we must not label anyone odd who gets excited about finding a new flower, a new path in the woods, or seeing an animal go through what seems to be a humorous routine.

Severe winters give the small animals and birds as difficult a time as it does humans. Have you ever seen a starnose mole in your own back yard burrow up through the snow under a bird feeder, snatch a seed of some kind, and run back to his own front door? One winter day the authors observed a small squirrel literally taking "super-animal" kangaroo hops through the foot deep snow. He would come up from nowhere, fly in a graceful arc, and disappear to get his footing for the next hop. Seven of these hops took so much energy that the muscles of the observing humans ached for the brave little guy. A knowing and understanding human being can appreciate the well earned relaxation that is evident when a beautiful squirrel's tail waves limply over the end of the tree nest as its owner naps. Looking out of your window on a cold winter day, have you ever seen a bluejay pick a special seed out of the feeder, fly to the nearest branch, transfer the seed from its beak to a toehold on the branch and then proceed to attack it with pneumatic drill precision to extract the choice bit inside? Or have you perhaps seen a squirrel attempt to do acrobatics to reach the feeder and fail in his high wire stunting? Or observed a pheasant stalking majestically through the deep snow, sinking breast deep with each step and presenting an unusual sight—"chicken scratching"—with his beautiful tail laid out on the snow? The storytelling opportunities in camp provide excellent means of relating true stories about the happenings in nature. The most cherished times in camp involve nature in some way. Camping cannot exist without the natural surroundings of the camp. Nature in camp should not be conducted as an isolated class.

Nature should be an active, doing part of each child's camp experience and not a book-ish, formal occasion. Every counselor should be alert for nature's interesting sideshows and should not hesitate to stop the work of the moment to point out the antics of a noisy jay, to try to figure out the age of a tree stump from its annual rings, or to watch a spider weave its web.

Conservation

Even counselors without much knowledge of nature have ample chance to teach respect for nature. Destruction of any form of wild life should be discouraged by impressing the camper with the interdependence of all plants and animals. True conservation is based upon an appreciation of the role each living thing plays in maintaining the balance of the whole.

Outward Bound and the American Youth Hostel are two organizations that share with organized camping in the acquisition of nature knowledges and outdoor living skills. Since camp locations provide a setting for a nature program, there are many ways to promote interest. Displays in prominent places, table displays, displays over the fireplace, a nature bulletin board, and labelled trees and flower plots would reach all campers. Specific projects in nature can be developed in the following ways: outdoor museums, nature hikes, nature games, nature photography, handicraft, dramatics (puppets, insect play, masks), notebooks, a bird cafeteria, collections, dance, songs, music, animal tracks, or flower shows.

Nature activities

Nature walks, unlike hikes, must be leisurely and for variety can include emphasis on smelling and listening, as well as on looking. Collections, rather than being ends in themselves, should give the child a chance to learn about the specimen's purpose, activity, value, and place in the balance of nature. Before removing the unusual specimen from its environment, care should be taken to see that ample quantities are left to carry on the species. A camera with a portrait attachment is valuable for preserving specimens that are better left intact. Insects, flowers, or small animals can often be raised or kept temporarily in camp. Crayon prints, spatter prints, or smoke prints of leaves make interesting rainy day activities. Small plaster casts of animal tracks, leaves, and flowers can be made by the more ambitious.

Nature games

Nature sounds. A particularly good game at night (perhaps before going to sleep on a camp out), which can take many forms, is one in which the participants listen to nature sounds and identify them.

What is it? A little imagination can produce many identification games in which the participants attempt to identify such things as pictures, written clues, or actual specimens. An interesting variation is a touch, taste, or smell identification game.

Nature was first. While not actually a game, this idea can be used to make campers aware of ways nature has for giving her creatures many of the conveniences we think of as human inventions. For example, the frog used watertight goggles long before men. He has transparent eyelids that roll up from the bottom for underwater use. The first canals were dug by beavers to float logs to their dam sites.

126

Active games

Nature-point race. The object of this game is to win the most points. Instead of saying go, the leader names something growing within sight and the players run to find the object, pick it up, and return with it to the leader.

Nature tag. This is a game played according to the standard tag rules except that there is more than one goal.

Alphabet hunt. The game is played in couples. Each couple is equipped with a pencil and paper with the alphabet on it. The object is to find, while walking, an object in nature beginning with each letter of the alphabet and record its name.

Nature treasure hunt. This is played in the same manner as regular treasure hunt except that notes are formed around descriptions of flowers or trees.

Nature race. Unobserved by the players, the leader places about twenty natural objects in a clear spot. These might be bark, leaves, bugs, rocks, and so on. The players are divided into small teams and line up behind a starting line a good distance from the spot where the objects are. On signal the players race to the objects (they can follow trail signs if the distance is lengthened even more), observe them in silence for one minute (a guard may be used), and after time is up, they race back to starting line and assemble in teams and make as complete a list of the objects as possible.

Matching leaves. At the first signal, everyone gathers one leaf from as many different types of trees as he can find. At the second whistle, the players return. The person with the largest number of different types of leaves, wins.

Inactive games

Are you? or *What am I?* (Twenty questions) The tree is it. The game is played with several small teams. The object is to find out what tree the player is by asking *indirect* questions to which he can answer yes or no. After each player has asked one question (up to a total of twenty), the teams retire to discuss the answers.

Chain spelling. The only words that can be used are those referring to something in nature. The players divide into two teams, which take turns spelling. The next object must begin with the last letter of the preceding word.

Hold your team. This is played with two teams. The object is to retain your players and obtain some from the other team. The leader holds up nature specimens and asks one team's first player for the name of it and the other team's first player for a fact about it. He reverses the order of the next identification by having team two identify it and team one give a fact. If a player misses, he goes to the other side, but the question remains the same until one of his team answers it.

I saw. This is a good game for summarizing and reviewing the work done on a field trip. The first player names an object that he observed on the trip and briefly describes it. The second player mentions the object described by number one and adds one observed by himself with a brief description.

The ability to enjoy nature does not require vast knowledge. Even the most experienced person can find enjoyment in the "feel" of a water-washed, sun-dried piece of wood; be delighted at discovering a Petosky stone, a sand dollar, or a starfish; or derive pleasure from creating a pine cone animal.

With nature crafts it is difficult to determine where the craft shops input begins or ends. Craft shops at camp need to be decommercialized in favor of natural media. Wood, stone, bark, seed pods, leaves and grasses, shells and clay are free and waiting to be used by the owner of an inventive mind. Creativeness knows no boundaries or limitations.

Tree test*

1. What tree do we put away in summer? (fur)
2. What tree remains after a fire? (ash)
3. Under what tree would you seek shelter from the rain? (umbrella tree)
4. What tree gave a nickname to an American general? (hickory)
5. What trees are always sad? (pine)
6. If asked by your best beau whom you loved, what tree would you give for an answer? (yew)
7. The old story tree? (chestnut)
8. The hero's tree? (laurel)
9. The quivering tree? (aspen)
10. What tree is a good church man? (elder)
11. What tree do you have in your hand? (palm)
12. The Garden of Eden tree? (apple)
13. What trees stick together? (gum)
14. What trees are always well dressed? (spruce)
15. What tree is part of a dress and a door? (hemlock)
16. What tree do we like stuffed? (olive)

Use display boxes on a wall in a prominent place. Keep each one filled every day with a single named specimen. Sometimes have a "what is it" drop box so that campers can identify the contents. An identification book can be nearby.

To touch each area in nature, the following assignments are made. The assignments will have to be changed to include specimens found in the locale of study. Draw a leaf of each of the following trees and indicate whether it is a hardwood or softwood tree.

Quaking aspen   Large toothed aspen

White oak   Red oak

Pin oak   Red maple

Canoe birch   Cherry birch

---

*The Cokesbury Game Book by Arthur M. Depew

White pine   Red pine

Jack pine   Tamarack (larch)

Balsam   Hemlock

Cedar   Juniper

    Flowers are grouped in families. Sketch the flower and the leaf and name the family to which it belongs.

These flowers form nature's carpet:

1.   3.

2.   4.

These flowers are rare in (name the state) and should not be picked.

1.   3.

2.   4.

These flowers are often confused due to their similarity to one another:

1.

2.

3.

These flowers have similar habitats and leaf shape.

1._____   2._____

This is a carnivorous plant.

1._____

Ferns grow on intimate terms with wildflowers. Write a few descriptive words about them:

Shrubs often provide food or drink. Name two, telling what they provide:

1.

2.

Moss is another of nature's carpets. Find two kinds, draw, and name them.

1.   2.

Record the names of the specimens that are placed in the nature display boxes.

Poisons in nature

Skin poisoning is caused most frequently by three plants: poison ivy, poison oak, and poison sumac. The ability to recognize these is the best guarantee of preventing the poisoning. List other poisons found in nature.

Birds

Birds are identified by their habitats (the place where you see them); their flight patterns (films are available); their plumage (films are available); and their song (records are available). A counselor should not be afraid to admit he does not know but should be quick to say, "Let's look it up." The study of birds need not be in a formal class presentation. Many teachable moments occur on hikes, taking canoe trips, during church services, awaking in the morning (especially on overnights), outside the cabin, and at feeding stations.

During the course of eight weeks learn to know two different kinds of birds found in each of the following habitats. Name the birds and tell briefly how you identified them.

1. Woodland

2. Field or meadow

3. Swamps or marshes

4. Lakeshore or ocean beach

Shells, fossils, minerals, rocks

As the camper walks along the water's edge there are many potential hobbies. Many of the objects found there can be used in displays, in crafts, in starting a hobby collection, in motivating a special interest group, or as the focal point of a story or a song. Select shells, fossils, minerals, or rocks and start to develop a plan that would motivate interest in informal study.

Animal tracks

In the early morning, especially after an overnight, animal tracks can be seen along the beach or bare earth in the woods. Draw a set of animal tracks that *you have seen* and tell how you decided to whom they belonged. Did you know these tracks could be collected? Plaster of Paris, a small brush, and a tin can without top or bottom are all it takes to collect them.

Insects

Insects are all around you. Observe one and write a short story about it.

Reptiles and amphibians

A counselor might just as well face the fact that a summer will not pass without an episode involving a snake, a frog, a toad, or a turtle. As a precaution, find out if there are poisonous snakes in your area and be able to recognize them if there are. Many adults' eyes shine a little brighter when they see Mr. Toad if they read Kenneth Graham's *The Wind in the Willows*. So will yours.

Is there a terrarium in your camp? Is it for cabin or community collections? Are there any tadpoles around? If you are going to have reptiles and amphibians around, the world of insects and small mammals will be within your reach. Why is this? Keep a record of how many times you encounter these "fellows" during the summer:

Snake
Frog
Toad
Turtle
Others

Stars

Stars are a subject on which an unlimited amount of time could be spent. Aside from the storytelling opportunities they provide, they suggest a great number of things to do. Briefly outline a project you believe would work in your camp.

There are "pointers" in the sky. These stars or groups of stars will help you find other groups.
1. The north star is in what constellation?
2. Where is the Little Dipper set in relation to the Big Dipper?
3. What constellation winds between the dippers?
4. The head of the dragon points to what constellation?
5. What constellation lies between the lady of the chair and the Little Dipper?
6. Corona Borealis lies where?
7. Arcturus is the large star in what constellation?

Space

The camp cannot ignore information from the outside world that filters into the campground via various routes. Most questions raised on hearing such information do not require highly scientific answers, and it does not seem too much to ask that counselors be aware of space travel, rockets, and satellites. The trip to the moon is no longer a legend. From the simple study of stars in camp can come the questions about astronomy that make counselors run and hide. Once again, it is only proper to admit that we do not know but will look it up and report back. It might be good to invite the camper to help.

Do you recognize the following words? Do you know what they mean? Payload, solid propellant, nozzle, throat, burning surface, combustion chamber, liquid propellant, retrofire, stages, Apollos, space walk, moon shot, Gemini, Mercury, pad, Mariner, UFO, and Freedom 7.

Fishing

In spite of the fact that most camps are situated on water, fishing is an activity that is frequently overlooked. There is no need to convince those who have already found the thrill of catching a "big" one, who have told about the one that got away, who have sat quietly observing the wonders of nature, who have had companionship in silence, and who have fallen into bed from a good feeling of fatigue for the best sleep they have ever had. Just in case you might be interested in initiating the unexperienced, beginning endeavors could fall into the following categories. Whether still fishing from a boat or pier for perch, blue gills, sunfish, catfish, bullheads, or bass, or trolling for pike, pickerel, or bass, standard equipment and bait will be needed. Suggested equipment include a drop line, pole and line, or casting rod, a tackle box, hooks, weights, and leaders. Bait might be worms, minnows, plugs, or bugs. If fishing while wading in streams for trout or white bass, the equipment and bait needed will vary somewhat. Suggested equipment includes fly rod, fly line, fly reel, fly leaders, boots or waders, a flybox landing net, creel, fly oil, line dressing, and scissors. Bait might be flies—wet, dry, or live.

Weather

In a camping environment the weather plays a vital part. All sorts of conjectures or guesses are made about it, so a simple study would be of interest and benefit to all.
1. How do clouds indicate weather?

2. What causes fog?

3. What causes dew?

4. What should you know about lightning and thunder?

Aids in predicting weather are wind direction, temperature readings, and barometer readings. Record the "old wives tales" you hear about weather. Comment on whether they are true or false.

List the weather observations you have made for the situation in which you are training.

Other activities

There are numerous other ways in which nature can be depicted. After the following activities indicate situations in which you see a potential for integrating the study of nature.

1. Dance

2. Games

3. Music

4. Singing

5. Dramatics

6. Crafts

Arts and crafts

Take the initiative.

The art program in any camp is an area not to be overlooked. A simple program can be just as satisfactory as an elaborate one. In many instances the camp environment provides natural materials that can be used in many ways. Look around you and list five "items of nature" (natural media) that could be worked into a craft project. Make suggestions for possible use.

1.

2.

3.

4.

5.

This program teaches one to work with others, to share ideas, tools, and materials. *Conversation* is a part of crafts. In addition an appreciation of the other persons' abilities is bound to develop. This appreciation will soon carry over into the other hours of the day. A hobby might develop from a simple craft experience. Crafts offer an opportunity for creative and original thinking and doing. There is definite relaxation for the individual who loses himself in the doing.

In starting such a program keep in mind that the craft room should be an inspiration. Perhaps a number of short-term projects using scrap materials would furnish opportunities for experimentation in the different media.

The crafts program does not stop at the door of the shop. There is hardly a part of the camp program that could not make use of the craft program. The needs may range from a simple poster to the scenery of a pageant or play. Because of this relationship with other departments, the materials and tools are often misused. Somehow everyone expects the craft shop to be open all the time.

Visit a craft room and make notes on the following:

1. What was being done in metal?

2. What was being done in leather?

3. What was being done in painting?

4. What was being done in drawing?

5. Make a list of the different media you have seen available in the craft shops.

Afterwards, try the following:

1. Use your "doodling" to create a design. Draw it below.

2. Fold a piece of paper and cut it at random. You might get a surprise.

3. Make an article in any media. Outline the steps involved in making this article.

If the cabin counselor or sports counselor comes to the craft shop and creates something, their interest enhances the appeal of these activities for the campers. Signs and "things" have to be made—for the cabin, the tournament on the bulletin board, the party, the skit, the songfest, the nature trail, and the dramatic program. Just to be able to sit and watch what and how the other fellow does it is most interesting and enlightening. Because of this precamp sessions should include a trip to the craft shop, direction on the procedures to be followed there, a look at the range of things that usually are done, and a warm invitation to come back anytime to watch, to work, or to help. Special sessions might even be held for counselors at a few scheduled times throughout the season.

Each item on the menu has been served. The campers and counselors linger a moment longer over their last bite and beverage to watch the sun dip lower into the water. The orange-red glow is as exciting to the counselor who has seen it for the hundredth time as it is to the camper seeing it for the first time. The important thing is that the group has seen the sunset together. This moment of awe somehow seems to pull everyone a little bit tighter together as a group because they have shared a special something. All are silent for just a moment longer and then someone says, "Who's on clean-up?" The spell is broken as everyone scrambles to answer the call to duty.

Suggested readings

GENERAL

Dimock, H., *The Administration of the Modern Camp*. New York: Association Press, 1949.

Dimock, H., and Statten, T., *Talks to Counsellors*. New York: Association Press, 1947.

Drought, A. R. *A Camping Manual*. New York: A. S. Barnes & Co., Inc., 1943.

Hammett, C., and Musselman, U. *The Camp Program Book*. New York: Association Press, 1951.

Joy, B. E. *Camping*. Minneapolis, Minn.: Burgess Publishing Company, 1957.

Mitchell, A. V., Crawford, I. B., and Rubberson, J. D. *Camp Counseling*. Philadelphia: W. B. Saunders Company, 1970.

Ott, E. *So You Want To Be A Camp Counselor*. New York: Association Press, 1949.

SPORTS

Ainsworth, D. *Individual Sports for Women.* Philadelphia: W. B. Saunders Company, 1955.

Division of Girls' and Women's Sports. Sport Guides. *Tennis and Badminton; Archery.*

Fait, H. F., Shaw, J. H., Fox, G. J., and Hollingsworth, C. B. *A Manual of Physical Education Activities.* Philadelphia: W. B. Saunders Company, 1956.

Myer, M. H., and Shwartz, M. M. *Team Sports for Women.* Philadelphia: W. B. Saunders Company, 1957.

Miller, D. M., and Lieg, K. L. *Individual and Team Sports For Women.* Englewood Cliffs, N. J.: Prentice Hall, Inc., 1955.

Mitchell, E. C. *Sports for Recreation and How to Play Them.* New York: The Ronald Press Company, 1952.

Orr, J. M. *A Manual of Riding.* Minneapolis, Minn.: Burgess Publishing Company, 1957.

Seaton, D. C., Clayton, I. A., Leibee, H. C., and Messersmith, L. *Physical Education Handbook.* Englewood Cliffs, N. J.: Prentice Hall, Inc., 1959.

Stephens, W. L. *Rifle Marksmanship.* New York: A. S. Barnes and Co., Inc., 1941.

Wilson, R. C. *Rifle Manual.* Minneapolis, Minn.: Burgess Publishing Company, 1946.

SPORTS (film strips:)

The Athletic Institute. Chicago, Ill.

Beginning archery

Beginning tennis

Beginning baseball

Beginning volleyball

Beginning badminton

Informal games

GAMES

Bancroft, J. H., *Games.* New York: Macmillan Publishing Co., Inc., 1946.

Keen, A. A. *The What To Do Book—Games and Pastimes for Younger Children.* Penn Publishing Co.

LaSalle, D. *Guidance of Children Through Physical Education.* New York: A. S. Barnes and Co., Inc., 1946.

Lawson, A. H. *Homemade Games.* Philadelphia: J. B. Lippincott Company, 1934.

MacFarlan, A. A. *New Games for 'Tween-agers.* New York: Association Press.

Marran, R. J. *Games Outdoors.* New York: Thomas Y. Crowell Company, Inc., 1940.

Mason, B., and Mitchell, E. *Active Games and Contests.* New York: A. S. Barnes and Co., Inc., 1935.

Richardson, H. *Games for the Elementary School Grades.* Minneapolis, Minn.: Burgess Publishing Company, 1957.

Richardson, H. A. *Games for Junior and Senior High School.* Minneapolis, Minn.: Burgess Publishing Company, 1957.

Smith, C. F. *Games and Game Leadership.* New York: Dodd, Mead and Company, 1932.

Staley, S. C. *Games, Contests, and Relays.* New York: A. S. Barnes and Co., Inc., 1924.

WATERFRONT

American National Red Cross. *Swimming and Water Safety.* Washington, D.C.

American National Red Cross. *Lifesaving and Water Safety.* Washington, D.C.

American National Red Cross. *Swimming Outlets.* Washington, D.C.

American National Red Cross. *Instructor's Manuals—Basic Courses in Canoeing, Outboard Boating, Rowing, Sailing.* Washington, D.C.

American National Red Cross. *Canoeing.* New York: Doubleday and Co.

Bearse, R. H., and Hazelton, S. C. *A Camp Aquatic Program.* Hanover, N.H.: S. C. Hazelton.

Brown, R. *Teaching Progression for the Swimming Instructor.* New York: A. S. Barnes and Co., Inc., 1948.

Cureton, T. K., Jr. *Fun In The Water.* New York: Association Press, 1948.

Curtiss, K. W. *Rhythmic Swimming.* Minneapolis, Minn.: Burgess Publishing Company, 1942.

Kiphuth, R. J. H. *Swimming.* New York: A. S. Barnes and Co., Inc., 1942.

Lukens, P. *Teaching Swimming.* Minneapolis, Minn.: Burgess Publishing Company, 1948.

New England Camping Association. *Canoeing Manual.* Boston.

Schneck, K. *Program Planning for the Camp Waterfront.* Allentown, Pa.: Jacobs and Bachman Press.

Seller, P., and Gundling, B. *Aquatic Art.* Cedar Rapids, Iowa: Adcraft.

Spears, B. *Beginning Synchronized Swimming.* Minneapolis, Minn.: Burgess Publishing Company, 1958.

PARTIES

Breen, M. J. *The Party Book.* New York: A. S. Barnes Co., Inc., 1939.

Carlson, B. W. *The Junior Party Book.* Nashville, Tenn.: Cokesbury Press.

DeMarche, E., and Davis. *Handbook of Co-Ed Teen Activities.* New York: Association Press.

Harowitz, J., and Harowitz, C. *A Treasury of Parties for Boys and Girls.* Hart Publishing Co., Inc., 1948.

Mason, B., and Mitchell, E. D. *Social Games for Recreation.* New York: The Ronald Press Company, 1935.

Parties Plus. New York: National Recreation Association.
  Let's Plan a Party
  Fun for Threesomes
  Stunts and Entertainment
  Parties for Special Days

DANCING

Duggan, A. S., and others. *Folk Dances of The United States and Mexico.* New York: The Ronald Press Co., 1948.

Duggan, A. S., Schottman, J., and Rutledge, A. *The Folk Dance Library.* New York: The Ronald Press Co., 1948.

Durlacher, editor. *Honor Your Partner,* New York: Devin-Adair Co., 1949.

Ford Foundation. *Good Morning.* Dearborn, Mich.

Harris, Swenson, and Pittman. *Dance a While.* Minneapolis, Minn.: Burgess Publishing Company, 1950.

Hostetler, L. *Walk Your Way to Better Dancing.* New York: The Ronald Press Company, 1952.

Price, M. K., *The Source Book of Play Party Games.* Minneapolis, Minn.: Burgess Publishing Company, 1949.

Ryan, G. *Dances of Our Pioneers.* New York: The Ronald Press Company, 1939.

Schonberg, H. *May I Have This Dance.* New York: Kamin Publishers, 1958.

Square Dances. Denver, Colo.: Foster's Folkway Features, 1942.

Tolman, and Page. *The Country Dance Book.* New York: A. S. Barnes and Co., Inc., 1937.

Waglow, I. F. *Social Dance for Students and Teachers.* William C. Brown Company, Publishers, 1953.

Weikart, P. *Syllabus-Workshop in Folk Dance.* Ann Arbor, Mich.: Department of Physical Education, University of Michigan.

MUSIC

Bower, E. *Recreation for Girls.* New York: A. S. Barnes & Co., Inc., 1934.

Commins, D. *Making an Orchestra.* New York: Macmillan Publishing Co., Inc., 1944.

Diller, A., and Page, D. S. *Rote Pieces for Rhythm Band.* G. Schirmer, Inc.

Huntington, H. *Tune Up.* New York: Doubleday, Doran and Co., 1942.

Waterman, E. *Rhythm Book.* New York: A. S. Barnes & Co., Inc., 1936.

CAMPFIRES

Burrows, M. *One Thousand and One Beautiful Things.* New York: Crown Publishers, Inc.

Hurley, R. J., *Campfire Tonight.* The Peak Press.

Jaeger, E. *Council Fires.* New York: Macmillan Publishing Co., Inc., 1949.

Smith, H. A. *The New Hymnal for American Youth.* Old Tappan, N.J.: Fleming H. Revell Company.

Welch, E. H. *Talks for Teenagers.* Minneapolis, Minn.: Burgess Publishing Company, 1959.

STORYTELLING

Association for Childhood Education. *Bibliography of Books for Children.* Washington, D.C.

Breen, M. J. *For The Story Teller.* New York: National Recreation Association, 1938.

Bryant, S. C., *How to Tell Stories To Children.* Boston: Houghton Mifflin Company.

Cowels, J. D., *The Art of Story Telling.* A. C. McClug & Co., 1914.

Ledlie, J., and Holbein, F. *The Camp Counselor's Manual.* New York: Association Press, 1946.

Sawyer, R. *The Way of the Story Teller.* New York: The Viking Press, 1942.

National Recreation Association. *Story Telling.* New York.

DRAMATICS

Eisenberg, H., and Eisenberg, L. *The Handbook of Skits and Stunts.* New York: Association Press, 1957.

CAMPFIRE BUILDING

Girl Scouts of America. *Girl Scout Handbook.*

Girl Scouts of America. *Campcraft A.B.C's.*

Joy, B. E. *Campcraft.* Minneapolis, Minn.: Burgess Publishing Company, 1957.

Mason. *The Book for Junior Woodsmen.*

Mason. *Woodcraft.*

Rutstrum, C. *Way of the Wilderness.* Minneapolis, Minn.: Burgess Publishing Company, 1946.

WOODCRAFT

Boy Scouts of America. *Handbook for Boys,* Jubilee edition.

Camp Fire Girls. *Out Door Book.*

Girl Scouts of America. *Girl Scout Handbook.*

Hammet, C. T. *Campcraft*. New York: Sandpiper Press, 1950.
Rutstrum, C. *Way of the Wilderness*. Minneapolis: Burgess Publishing Company, 1946.

NATURE

Collingwood, C. H., and Brush, W. D. *Knowing Your Trees*. Washington, D.C.: The American Forestry Association, 1947.
Ickis, M. *Nature in Recreation*. New York: A. S. Barnes and Co., Inc., 1938.
Limbach, R. T., and Everett, T. H. *American Trees*. New York: Random House, Inc., 1942.
Marx, D. S. *Learn the Trees From Leaf Prints*. Cincinnati, Ohio: The Boston Publishing Co., 1938.
Peattie, D. C. *Trees You Want to Know*. Racine, Wis.: Whitman Publishing Co., 1934.
Zim, H. S., and Martin, A. *Trees*. New York: Simon & Schuster, Inc., 1952.

WILDFLOWERS

Aiken, G. D. *Pioneering With Wild Flowers*. New York: Stephen Daye Press, 1946.
Harvey, J. *Wild Flowers of America*. Racine, Wis.: Whitman Publishing Co., 1932.
Hausman, E., *Beginners Guide to Wild Flowers*. New York: G. P. Putnam's Sons, 1948.
Hausman, E. *Encyclopedia of American Wild Flowers*. New York: Garden City Publishing Company, 1947.
House, H. D. *Wild Flowers*. New York: MacMillan Publishing Co., Inc., 1934. Reprint 1961.
Mathews, F. *A Book of Wild Flowers for Young People*. New York: G. P. Putnam's Sons, 1923.
Matschat, C. H. *American Wild Flowers*. New York: Random House, Inc., 1940.
McKenny, M. *A Book of Wild Flowers*. New York: Macmillan Publishing Co., Inc., 1939.
Rosner, J. *Let's go for a Nature Walk*. New York: G. P. Putnam's Sons, 1959.
Wherry, E. *Wild Flower Guide*. New York: Doubleday & Company, Inc., 1948.
Zim, H. S., and Martin, A. *Flowers*. New York: Simon & Schuster, Inc., 1950.

FERNS AND MOSSES

Clute, W. N. *Our Ferns*. New York: Frederick Stokes Co., 1939.
Conard, H. *How to Know Mosses*. Mt. Pleasant, Iowa: H. E. Jaques, 1944.
Dunham, E. *How to Know Your Mosses*. New York: Houghton Mifflin Company, 1916.
Durand, H. *Field Book of Common Ferns*. New York: G. P. Putnam's Sons, 1928.
Hattes, A. *The Book of Shrubs*. A. T. De La Mare Co., 1929.
Keeler, H. *Our Northern Shrubs*. Charles Scribner's Sons, 1935.
Wiley, F. A. *Ferns of Northeastern United States*. New York: Dover Publications, Inc., 1973.

POISONS IN NATURE

Jaeger, E. *Wildwood Wisdom*. New York: Macmillan Publishing Co., Inc., 1945.

NATURE STUDY—BIRDS

Cornell University Laboratory of Ornithology. *American Bird Songs*. Ithaca, N.Y.: Comstock Publishing Associates.
Hausman, L. *Encyclopedia of American Birds*. Garden City, N.Y. Garden City Publishing Co.
Peterson, R. T. *Bird Study*. New York: Boy Scouts of America, 1938.
Peterson, R. T. *A Field Guide to Birds*. New York: Houghton Mifflin Company, 1939.
Zim, H. S., and Gabrielson, I. *Birds*. New York: Golden Press, 1949.

NATURE STUDY—ROCKS AND MINERALS

Dana, E. S. *Minerals and How to Study Them*. John Wiley & Sons, Inc., 1949.
Loomis, F. B. *Field Book of Common Rocks and Minerals*. G. P. Putnam's Sons, 1948.
O'Connell, D. T. *Rocks and Minerals*. New York: Boy Scouts of America Merit Badge Series.
Pearl, R. M. *How to Know the Minerals and Rocks*. New York: The New American Library, Inc., 1957.
Zim, H. S., and Shaffer, P. A. *Rocks and Minerals*. New York: Golden Press, 1957.
Zim, H. S., and Ingle, L. *Seashores*. New York: Golden Press, 1955.

NATURE STUDY—ANIMALS

Schmidt, K. P. *Homes and Habits of Wild Animals*. Chicago and New York: M. A. Donohue Co., 1934.
Stalking, New York: Boy Scouts of America Merit Badge Series.
Zim, H. S., Hoffmeister, D. F., and Irving, J. *Mammals*. New York: Golden Press, 1955.

NATURE STUDY—INSECTS

Bradley, C. J., and Palmer, E. L. *Insect Life*. New York: Boy Scouts of America Merit Badge Series.
Conrad, H. *How to Know Insects*. Mt. Pleasant, Iowa: H. E. Jaques, 1944.
Fazzeni, L. D. *Insects of America*. Racine, Wis.: Whitman Publishing Co., 1937.

Fazzeni, L. D. *Butterflies and Moths*. Racine, Wis.: Whitman Publishing Co., 1934.
Tortal, C. *The Life of a Queen Bee*. New York: A Venture Book.
Zim, H. S., Cottam, C., and Irving, J. G. *Insects*. New York: Simon & Schuster, Inc., 1951.

NATURE STUDY—REPTILES AND AMPHIBIANS
Grahame, K. *The Wind in the Willows*. New York: The Heritage Press, 1940.
Zim, H. S., and Smith, H. M. *Reptiles and Amphibians*. New York: Simon & Schuster, Inc., 1956.

ASTRONOMY
Bernhard, Bennett, and Rice. *New Handbook of Heavens*. New York: McGraw-Hill Book Company, 1941.
Newell, H. E., Jr. *Space Book for Young People*. New York: McGraw-Hill Book Company, 1958.
Olcott, W., and Putman, A. W. *Field Book of Skies*. New York: G. P. Putnam's Sons, 1934.
Olcott, W. *Book of the Stars for Young People*. New York: G. P. Putnam's Sons, 1923.
Zim, H. S., Baker, R. H., and Irving, J. G. *Stars*. New York: Golden Press, 1951.

FISHING
Bergman, R. *With Fly Plug and Bait*. New York: William Morrow & Co., Inc., 1947.
Zim, H. S., and Shoemaker, H. H. *Fishes*. New York: Simon & Schuster, Inc., 1956.

WEATHER
Lehr, P. E., Burnett, R. W., Zim, H. S., and McNaught, H. *Weather*. New York: Simon & Schuster, Inc., 1957.
Mitchell, A. V., and Crawford, I. B. *Camp Counseling*. Philadelphia: W. B. Saunders Company, 1961.
Schneider, H. *Everyday Weather—How it Works*. New York: McGraw-Hill Book Company, 1961.

CRAFTS IN NATURE
Bale, R. O. *Creative Nature Crafts*. Minneapolis, Minn.: Burgess Publishing Company, 1959.

CRAFTS
Art Activities Almanac. Detroit, Mich.: Wayne State University.
Hammett, C. T., and Horrocks, C. M. *Creative Crafts for Campers*. New York: Association Press.
Ickis, M., and Esh, E. S. *The Book of Arts and Crafts*. New York: Associated Press, 1957.
Leeming, J. *Fun with Plastics*. Philadelphia, Pa.: J. B. Lippincott Company, 1946.
McLeish, M. *Beginnings: Teaching Arts to Children*. London and New York: The Studio Publications, Inc., 1941.
Perry, E. K. *Crafts for Fun*. New York: William Morrow and Co., Inc., 1940.
Reynolds, A. H. *Low Cost Crafts for Everyone*. New York: Blue Ribbon Books, 1943.
Shanklin, M. E. *Use of Native Craft Material*. Peoria, Ill.: Manual Arts Press, 1947.
Spears, M. *Keeping Idle Hands Busy*. Minneapolis, Minn.: Burgess Publishing Company, 1950.
Staples, F. *Arts and Crafts for the Recreation Leader*. New York: Associated Press, 1943.
Tomlinson, R. R. *Crafts For Children*. London and New York: The Study Publications.

CRAFT SUPPLY SOURCES
Tandy Leather Company
4823 Woodward Avenue
Detroit, Michigan

The Copper Shop (enameling products)
2185 E. 14th Street
Cleveland 15, Ohio

American Handicrafts Co.
83 W. Van Buren Street
Chicago, 5, Illinois

Cleveland Crafts of Ohio
4707 Euclid Avenue
Cleveland 3, Ohio

Dearborn Leather Company (best leather)
8625 Linwood Avenue
Detroit 6, Michigan

Magnus Craft Materials, Inc.
108 Franklin Street
New York 13, N.Y.

Vanity Fair (copper findings)
Box 991
Evanston, Illinois

The Handcrafters (wood products)
Waupun, Wisconsin

Additional readings

GENERAL

American Camping Association, Inc. *Publications and Selected Resources*. Martinsville, Ind.: The Association, 1963.

Joy, B. E. *Annotated Bibliography of Camping*. Minneapolis, Minn.: Burgess Publishing Company, 1963.

Mitchell, A., and Crawford, I. B. *Camp Counseling*. Philadelphia: W. B. Saunders Company, 1961.

AQUATICS

Allen, J. J. *Boating/A Beginning Guide*. New York: The Ronald Press Company, 1958.

American National Red Cross. Washington, D.C.
Canoeing
Swimming and Diving
Swimming for the Handicapped
Aquatic Games, Pageants and Stunts. New York: Hoffman-Harris, Inc. 1947.

Boys' Clubs of America. *Water Stunts*. New York.

Gabrielsen, M., Spears, B., and Gabrielsen, B. *Aquatic Handbook*. Englewood Cliffs, N.J.: Prentice-Hall, Inc., 1960.

Mann, M., and Fries, C. C. *Swimming Fundamentals*. Englewood Cliffs, N.J.: Prentice-Hall, Inc., 1949.

Schneck, R. *Program Planning for the Camp Waterfront*. Allenton, Pa.: Jacobs and Buchman Press, 1952.

Spears, B. *Beginning Synchronized Swimming*. Minneapolis, Minn.: Burgess Publishing Company, 1950.

CRAFTS

Bale, R. O. *Creative Nature Crafts*. Minneapolis, Minn.: Burgess Publishing Company, 1959.

Hening, V. *Fun with Scraps*. Beverly Hills, Calif.: Bruce Publishing Company, 1947.

NATURE

Bale, R. O. *Stepping Stones to Nature*. Minneapolis, Minn.: Burgess Publishing Company, 1960.

Craig, G. S., and Hurley, B. D. *Exploring in Science*. Lexington, Mass.: Ginn and Company, 1960.

Fabre, J. H. *The Story-Book of Science*. New York: Appleton-Century-Crofts.

Gaudette, M. E. *Leader's Nature Guide*. Girl Scouts of America.

Hylander, C. J. *Out of Doors in Summer*. New York: Macmillan Publishing Co., Inc.

Jaeger, E. *Nature Crafts*. New York: Macmillian Publishing Co., Inc., 1947.

Madden, I. C. *Creative Handicraft*. Chicago: The Goodheart-Willcox Company, 1955.

Nickelsburg, *The Nature Program at Camp*. Minneapolis, Minn.: Burgess Publishing Company.

Patch, E. M. *Holiday Pond*. New York: Macmillan Publishing Co., Inc., 1929.

Price, B. *Adventuring in Nature*. National Recreation Association, 1939.

SPORTS

Ainsworth, D. *Individual Sports for Women*, Philadelphia: W. B. Saunders Company, 1955.

*Fait, M., Shaw, J., Fox, and Hollingsworth, C. *A Manual of Physical Education Activities*. Philadelphia: W. B. Saunders Company, 1961.

Meyer, M. H., and Schwartz, M. *Team Sports for the Girls and Women*. Philadelphia: W. B. Saunders Company, 1957.

Miller, D. M., and Ley, L. *Individual and Team Sports for Women*. Englewood Cliffs, N.J.: Prentice-Hall, Inc., 1955.

*Mitchell, E., editor. *Sports for Recreation*. New York: The Ronald Press Company, 1952.

Seaton, C., and Leibee, M. *Physical Education Handbook*. Englewood Cliffs, N. J.: Prentice-Hall, Inc., 1959.

*Stanley, D. K., and Waglow, I. F. *Physical Education Handbook*. Boston: Allyn & Bacon, Inc., 1962.

Sports Skills. Belmont, Calif. Wadsworth Publishing Company.
Beginning Archery. Niemeyer, R.
Beginning Badminton. Friedrich, J., and Rutledge, A.
Beginning Bowling. Casady, D. R., and Liba, M. R.
Beginning Golf. Bruce, B. F., and Davies, E.
Beginning Handball. Roberson, R., and Olson, H.
Beginning Swimming. Mackenzie M., and Spears, B.
Beginning Tennis. Everett, P., and Dumas, V.
Beginning Volleyball. Odeneal, W. T., and Wilson, H. E.
These books offer excellent basic materials on the respective sports—including history, equipment, techniques, rules, testing program, glossary, self-testing and evaluation, and bibliography.

Wilson Sporting Goods Company. *Athletic Field and Court Diagrams*.

*Authors have focused on coeducational use.

The following organizations publish annual rule books for boys and men in football, baseball, basketball, track and field, and swimming.

N.C.A.A. and National Federation of State High School Athletic Associations
7 S. Dearborn St.
Chicago, Ill.

National Collegiate Athletic Bureau
Box 757, Grand Central Station
New York, N.Y.

Guides containing official playing rules for girls and women, as well as articles on techniques, teaching, organization, bibliographies, and so on, are also available. Sports covered are aquatics, archery and riding, bowling and fencing, golf, field hockey and lacrosse, soccer and speedball, softball, tennis and badminton, track and field, volleyball, winter sports, and outing activities. They are published every two years by the National Association for Girls and Women's Sports, 1201 Sixteenth St. N. W., Washington, D.C.

part V

reports and records

Honesty is the best policy

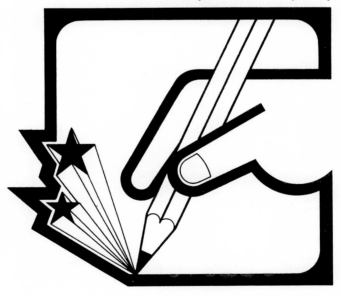

Camping involves many written records and reports. In most cases they are designed within the camp itself. In some instances standard reports are shared by all camps, and in others the camp is obligated to use forms from certain outside agencies. Many counselors are not aware of such obligations. Through a designated department, states will require an application form to set up the camp. This is followed up by a yearly record form. Inspections by authorized state people are recorded on forms. Sanitation reports for the health department are standard procedures and are essential. The American Camping Association has instituted the practice of camp inspection or visitation for the purpose of keeping up on improving the standards. Record the addresses of the agencies within your state that are involved in the licensing and inspection of camps. Are they governmental, voluntary, or mandatory?

The American Camping Association,* founded in 1935, is organized at national, regional, and state levels. The official publication is the Camping Magazine. The following publications are available from the Association:

Camp Standards with interpretation for the accreditation of Organized Camps (revised 1975)
National Directory of Accredited Camps for Boys and Girls (1975)
Yearly catalog of selected camping publications.

Records originating within the camp are campers' applications; staff applications; financial records, which can be broken down into specific areas such as equipment purchase, food, salaries, improvement of facilities, and upkeep of facilities; progress reports on campers; final reports on campers; and evaluations of personnel. Make a collection of these forms.

Suggestions for the director

Practice what you preach.

In preparing for the summer the director can develop three aids to help the counselor or counselor-in-training feel more secure. These are (1) a counselor's manual pertaining to the specific camp; (2) a precamp training period or workshop; and (3) planned in-service training.

Counselor's manual

Printed information about the camp, the job, the rules, and the traditions is welcomed by a CIT or a counselor new to a camp. It should be in the hands of the counselor *before* coming to camp and can serve as a manual during any precamp training period. Reports written by immediate predecessors also are enlightening. Counselors like to come prepared with source material. They should know the source books available in camp.

A suggested outline of information to be presented to new counselors follows:
1. A word of welcome from director
2. Objectives of the camp
3. Location
   a. How to get there by car, bus, plane, train
   b. How to label and mark baggage
   c. Mailing address
   d. Map of camp

---

*American Camping Association, Inc., Bradford Woods, Martinsville, Indiana 46151.

4. Short history of camp
5. Diagram of administration
6. The counselor's job
    a. call attention to first week adjustments of campers
    b. health procedures
    c. visitors' day
    d. reports and evaluations
    e. safety rules
7. Waterfront, fire precautions, and so on
8. Necessary articles
    a. list of articles
    b. description of uniform, where to get it, laundry arrangements
9. Counselor behavior, in camp, out of camp, and during free time

Precamp training period or workshop

This kind of work period is being used more and more by camp directors. It allows time to set the stage before the arrival of the campers. New personnel have a chance to get acquainted with returning personnel and to get oriented to the camp. *A counselor must feel secure in his position to be of help to the campers.* The length of the precamp varies according to the size of the camp and the amount of work to be done. One day to a full week may be needed prior to the arrival of the campers.

Questions always arise as to how much of the labor involved in opening the camp should fall to the counselors and whether time in the precamp period should be allotted for this work. The major allotment of time should be used for discussion relevant to handling the campers and to problems that are bound to arise. Ample time should be allowed the counselor for reading application blanks, campers' records, reports, to ask questions about the job, and to make individual preparations for specific activities, such as putting the craft room in order, readying the waterfront, arranging the library, setting up play areas, and making charts. There should be a minimum of menial tasks and provision should be made for others to do all heavy lifting. In the work period there should be opportunity for a bit of recreation and relaxation. If the camp personnel do some camp activities together, such as a campfire, cook-out, or overnight, a better understanding and rapport should result. It gives the director an opportunity to observe a counselor's skills. It gives the counselor a chance to review skills and become better acquainted with the director.

The following is an outline for a four-day precamp session:

First day
1. Arrival of new counseling personnel (they stay together in one cabin)
2. Basic administrative personnel and new counselors discuss:
    a. objectives
    b. history and traditions
    c. chain-of-command
    d. general rules
3. Director goes over specific job in personal interview
4. Question period
5. Recreation period
6. Tour of grounds

Second day
1. Arrival of returning personnel

2. Get-acquainted period
3. Assignment of cabins and getting settled
4. Review of information on campers and work with divisional director
5. Discussion period
6. Recreational period
7. Campfire and learning traditional camp songs

Third day
1. Explanation of program
2. Explanation of activities
3. Development of a master chart of special events
4. Swim tests and canoe tests
5. Question period
6. Cookout and overnight or sleepout

Fourth day
1. Cabins in readiness
2. Go over camper information; know names and faces if possible
3. Recreation areas in readiness
4. Swim
5. Shoreline exploration in canoes and picnic supper
6. Get a good night's sleep!

To close a workshop or training session on an inspirational note, send each person on his way with "determined thoughts of doing" or at least wondering why they have put themselves in this position for a whole summer. A sample of an appropriate closing follows:

My creed

This is my creed: "To live each day as though I may never see the morrow come; to give the advantage, but never ask for it; to be kindly to all, but kinder to the less fortunate; to respect all honest employment; to remember always that my life is made easier and better by the service of others; and to be grateful. To be tolerant and never arrogant; to treat all men with equal courtesy; to be true to my own in all things; to make as much as I can of my strength and the day's opportunity; and to meet disappointment without resentment. To be friendly and helpful whenever possible; to do without display of temper or bitterness, all that fair conduct demands; and to keep my money free from cunning or the shame of a hard bargain; to govern my actions so that I may fear neither reproach nor misunderstanding, nor words of malice or envy; and to maintain, at whatever temporary cost, my own self-respect. This is my Creed and my philosophy. I have failed it often and shall fail it many times again; but by these teachings I have lived to the best of my ability; laughed often, loved, suffered, grieved, found consolation, and have prospered. By friendships I have been enriched, and the home I have built has been happy.

Anonymous

Suggestions for the CIT
Information about your camp

1. What is the method of licensing in your state? (governmental, child agency, good handling)

2. Are there follow-up visits after the first year of operation?

3. What governmental agencies are involved in the inspection?

4. What federal legislation affects the operation of the camp?

5. What different forms and reports is a counselor called upon to do?

6. List other types of records not mentioned above:

   (File sample of record and report forms in this section.)
7. Record the tasks expected of you in the closing of camp after the camper has gone.

Example of a form that could be used by a CIT
for a visit to another camp

1. **General**

   Name of camp _____ Date _____

   Summer address _____

   Director's name _____

   Ownership: (check one) Private _____ Public agency _____

   Private agency _____ Length of season _____ Number of periods per season _____ Type
   of camp (i.e. sports, crippled children, speech correction, music, etc.)

   _____

   Objectives of the camp: _____

   _____

   _____

   _____

2. **Camper**

   Age of campers _____ Sex of campers _____

   Total number of campers _____ How are campers selected? _____

   _____

   On what basis is a camper placed in cabin group? _____

   _____

   How many campers are there in a group? _____

   How many groups in a unit or section? _____

   On what basis is camper placed in activities? _____

   _____

   Approximately how much time daily does a camper spend in:

   All camp activities _____ "Free play" _____ Small group activity _____ Unit or section

   activity _____ Lone activities _____?

3. **Camp site**

   The approximate acreage in wooded area is _____; in clear area _____.
   Is there access to water suitable for swimming, boating, and waterfront activities?

   _____

   The distance of the site from densely populated areas is _____.

4. **Equipment**

   The sleeping quarters provided are: (check)

   Dormitories _____ Tents_____ Cabins _____

   Size of same _____ Number of same _____ Number of campers accommodated in one

   tent or cabin _____

Continued.

Number of tents or cabins in one unit or section _____

The water safety equipment provided is _____

_____

The fire protection equipment provided is _____

_____

Is there: Indoor recreation space? _____ An office or administration quarters?

Dispensary? ____ Isolation unit? _____

Counselor's retreat? _____ Screened-in dining space? _____

5. **Camp program**
How much emphasis is placed on the following activities in the various camp program areas:

a. *Waterfront*

	None	Little	Some	Much
Swimming	_____	_____	_____	_____
Canoeing	_____	_____	_____	_____
Rowing	_____	_____	_____	_____
Sailing	_____	_____	_____	_____
Canoe trips	_____	_____	_____	_____
Boat trips	_____	_____	_____	_____

b. *Social recreation*

	None	Little	Some	Much
Campfire programs	_____	_____	_____	_____
Parties	_____	_____	_____	_____
Movies	_____	_____	_____	_____
Dancing	_____	_____	_____	_____
Games	_____	_____	_____	_____
Song fests	_____	_____	_____	_____
Story telling	_____	_____	_____	_____
Dramatics	_____	_____	_____	_____

c. *Camp craft*

	None	Little	Some	Much
Hikes	_____	_____	_____	_____
Cookouts	_____	_____	_____	_____
Sleepouts	_____	_____	_____	_____
Trail blazing	_____	_____	_____	_____
Woodcraft	_____	_____	_____	_____
First aid	_____	_____	_____	_____
Firebuilding	_____	_____	_____	_____

Continued.

	None	Little	Some	Much
d. *Arts and crafts*				
Metal craft				
Leather craft				
Ceramics and pottery				
Painting				
Drawing				
Woodwork				
Weaving				
List others below				
e. *Out-of-doors or nature*				
Trees				
Wild flowers				
Stars				
Birds				
Shells and fossils				
Insects				
List others below				
f. *Physical recreation*				
Baseball				
Archery				
Tennis				
Riding				
Badminton				
Football				
Basketball				
Volleyball				
List others below				

Continued.

g. In what ways do campers share in the program planning? _____

_____

6. **Personnel**

Number employed

a. *Classification*

Directors _____

Assistant directors or unit leaders _____

Program directors _____

Nurses _____

Doctors _____

Activities directors (do not have cabin group respon- _____
sibility)

Counselors with only cabin group leadership respon- _____
sibility

Counselors with other program of activity duties in _____
addition to cabin group leadership responsibility

Other staff members (cooks, clerks, etc.) _____

b. *What methods are used in selecting camp personnel?*   *Check*

A counselor and staff application form _____

Personnel interview _____

References _____

Passing health and skill tests _____

List other means of selection below _____

_____

_____

c. Are all members of camp personnel required to sign a written agreement? ___

7. **Health**

Is a physical examination required of all staff members before arrival at camp? ___

Is there a check of campers by a nurse or doctor upon arrival at camp? _____

Is there a rest period each day for campers? How long? _____ How is it ob-

served? _____

_____

List other health measures that you have observed. _____

_____

_____

ABC's for the CIT

Age characteristics
Boys
Campcraft
Drama
Effort
First aid
Girls
Handicraft
Intelligence
Justice
Kindliness
Love
Maturity
Nature
Objectivity
Patience
Questions
Reports
Sports
Truthfulness
Uniqueness
Vivacity
Waterfront
Xcellence
You
Zeal

index